The author as a 12-year-old

ALSO BY MIKE KELLY

FICTION

Technical Difficulties

With Hope Comes Pain

NONFICTION

Special Stories: Short Stories On Youth With Disabilities And My Adventures Working In The Disabilities Field

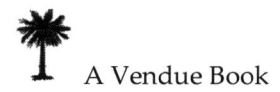

GRAY SKIES
A (Moron's) Memoir

Mike Kelly

A Vendue Book

GRAY SKIES: A (Moron's) Memoir

Copyright © MMXIX by Mike Kelly

All rights reserved. No part of this book may be reproduced or transmitted in any form or by any means, electronic or mechanical, including photocopying, recording, or by any information storage and retrieval system without expressed permission in writing from the author, except for brief quotations used in articles and reviews.

First printing
Printed and bound in the United States of America

Kelly, Mike
GRAY SKIES: A (Moron's) Memoir, Nonfiction

ISBN 978-0-9974352-6-9 (Paperback)
ISBN 978-0-9974352-7-6 (E-book)
ISBN 978-0-9974352-8-3 (Hardcover)
Library of Congress Control Number: 2018909534

A Vendue Book

1. Biography & Autobiography—Nonfiction.   2. Personal Memoirs—Nonfiction.   3. Humor

For information on GRAY SKIES: A (Moron's) Memoir, visit
www.venduebooks.com

© Photos of author as youth courtesy of William J. Safuontis

10 9 8 7 6 5 4 3 2 1 7 2 8 2 9 2 1 7 2 9 2 6 – **GY-2**

For my mother

and Ernie

This book is a memoir. It reflects the author's present recollections of experiences while growing up a moron and reflects his opinions relating to those experiences. Some names, places, and characteristics have been changed, some events have been compressed, and some dialogue has been re-created.

PROLOGUE

The great social reformer Frederick Douglass declared, "It is easier to build strong children than to repair broken men."

As a repaired broken man, I could not agree more. When you're a child and trying to figure out who you are, where you fit into this crazy world, and why your face and feelings are all a mess—and a zillion other thoughts—it's not the most encouraging thing to be told by your mother that your entry into this world was an accident. But that's exactly what my mom, God rest her Catholic soul, told me when I was fourteen. Confused, I asked if by 'accident' she meant that my father slipped on a banana peel and landed into her while he was in a state of arousal. My mother scrunched her face and gave me the deadeye stare, saying she didn't mean *that*. She suggested I was *unplanned*.

Whew, what a relief! In a flash, my status was upgraded from accident to unplanned. Uh, thank you?

My mother, Patricia, was a maverick and a hoot. She was a gritty New Yorker raised during the Great Depression. A Renaissance woman, she graduated from college during a time when most women didn't even go, and she told it unfiltered as she saw it. Whether it hurt your feelings or not was irrelevant.

I recall when I was seventeen and arrived home from high school one day to find photos of Brother 2, three years my senior, in various poses, spread out over the kitchen table. Curious, I asked my mom what they were. She said they were headshots of Brother 2. I inquired where they came from and why she had them. My mother said Brother 2 looked like a model, so she paid to have a photographer take photos of him to send to modeling agencies in Manhattan. Jealous, I asked my mother why she hadn't gotten any headshots of me. Without skipping a beat, she ruefully replied with a straight face, "Because you don't look like a model."

She didn't mince words, that's for sure. But her words stung. After a moment of open-mouthed stare, I shot back, "Well, everyone always says I look just like you, Mom."

It's a wonder how I ever developed any self-esteem and confidence at all, considering my closest parent thought I was not good-looking. Well, at least not as handsome as Brother 2. It's another wonder how I was able to achieve success in life in anything, considering my mom thought I was a moron. Yeah, that's right—a moron.

I tried to look at the bright side, though. My mother thinking I was a moron could have been a compliment. You see, there's a hierarchy of intellectual capacities: that being an imbecile, idiot, and moron. Of the three, a moron has the highest intelligence level (IQ of 51-70). An idiot has the lowest (IQ of 0-25). An imbecile lies in the middle (IQ of 26-50). It could've been worse. My mother could have thought I was an imbecile or an idiot!

What made her think I was a moron? Up through the seventh grade, I was an A student, with a B rarely appearing on my report cards. When I turned fourteen, in the eighth grade, things suddenly and inexplicably changed in my brain. Though I could still read at the top level of my class, I had great difficulty comprehending the words I'd read. I also struggled to focus my attention. I was beside myself with those two deficits. Years later, when I became a special educator working with youth with various types of challenges, I realized I had learning disabilities as a child. It was as if the door to a thirty-year unsolved mystery had been unlocked.

Learning disabilities in children are common nowadays, as there's an acronym for just about every type of challenge: ADD, ADHD, OCD, ODD, BD, ED, OH, PDD, and so on, with all sorts of accommodations for kids with learning differences. But going to a Catholic school in the 1970s, there were no such acronyms, and I was afforded no such accommodations. I'd get a smack on the skull from one of the angry nuns and be chided to stop daydreaming and pay better attention. Then I'd go home and get another smack on my head from my angry dad, asking me if I had rocks in my head and why I wasn't paying attention in class. As a kid, I thought I'd grow up to become a geologist. My father often said I had rocks in my head. *It made sense,* I thought. Some nuns at my Catholic grammar school told me the same thing, usually after hitting me on that same skull. I wasn't sure what all the hitting was about. I once asked my mother if I was a piñata. She said no, I was a little boy and questioned why I asked her such a ridiculous thing. I demanded to know why I was getting smacked around like a piñata by the nuns holding pointers, paddles, rulers, or anything else they could get their holy hands on. My mother shot me a look and didn't answer. A loyal Catholic schoolgirl, she sided with the sisters. I swear, I still have dents in my head from those crazy nuns. I watch

UFC fighters get hit fewer times than I saw schoolboys get walloped in their noggins by the sisters in Catholic school back then. It's possible that those ill-tempered women were in the wrong line of work. Frankly, I think they should've been prize fighters. The pay was better.

When I transitioned into high school, my reading comprehension issues and academic struggles worsened. As a result, I lost interest in school and focused on music, mischief, sports, and girls—in that order. My grades slipped to Ds, and I barely graduated from high school. So that was what was imprinted on my mother's brain; herself a straight-A student throughout high school and college—graduating summa cum laude from her Catholic university. How could it be that she gave birth to a D-student in high school: *a moron*?

Years later, when I began dating a beautiful, intelligent girl who'd eventually become my wife, I introduced her to my mother. The first question my mother asked my then-girlfriend—and now wife of 24 years—was what college she graduated from.

Interesting first question. As opposed to Where are you from? Where do you live? How did you meet my son? Where did you buy that nice blouse?

But, hey, that was my mom. Why beat around the bush when you can cut right to the chase?

My girlfriend replied the College of William and Mary in Williamsburg, Virginia. My mother's face lit up like a Christmas tree, and her eyes grew large. She complimented my girlfriend, remarking it was the second oldest college in America after Harvard, with Thomas Jefferson as its most distinguished graduate.

My girlfriend smiled and nodded, impressed with the knowledge and appreciating the recognition. After a moment of joy, my mother turned her head to me with a puzzled look.

"Hmm," she uttered.

Fortunately for me at the time, my future wife politely excused herself to visit the bathroom. Maybe she sensed what was coming. Now that I was alone with mom, I pounced.

"What does 'hmm' mean?" I questioned in a whispered voice.

"Oh, nothing. It's just that . . . never mind."

"Come on . . . let it out."

"Well, you always seem to date intelligent girls: the medical doctor, that psychotherapist with the wild hair, the MIT scientist, and now this young lady from such a prestigious college." The poor thing looked baffled as if she were trying to interpret a language she did not speak. "I just think it's interesting. You barely made it out of high school and dropped out of college, soooo. . ."

I rolled my eyes. "I see what you're saying," I snapped back. "But don't you think it's within the realm of possibility that I date intelligent women because I actually *am* smart, and the women find me intelligent?"

With a straight face, she replied, "No."

My future wife returned from the bathroom and saw my stunned expression.

That was what my mother thought of me.

And my father? Well, if he even thought of me at all—which is debatable—it was not as highly as my mother thought, that's for sure. You'll read about him later.

My sister—thirteen years my senior—didn't even look at me until I was a month old, claimed my mother. She already had two younger brothers and desperately wanted a little sister, yet got me instead.

My family was a mess, like many families, I suppose. But its beginnings had all the promise of great success.

My parents were bright and college-educated. In fact, my father once attended medical school before dropping out to work full-time after getting married.

I guess the day he left medical school was when things started turning south for my parents. My dad, a mathematician and extreme introvert, probably never should have married and had children. But he got married and had four kids: three planned and one accident.

That's me, the accident. And this is my story.

CHAPTER 1

An Accident Waiting To Happen

My parents were New Yorkers: my mother was born and raised in Midtown Manhattan's Hell's Kitchen neighborhood, and my father in the Spanish Harlem neighborhood. They were raised during the Great Depression, met at a Catholic school dance in 1949, and began dating. My dad was in medical school then, and my mother thought she'd won the life lottery; she would marry a doctor. Jackpot! Little did that naive twenty-one-year-old know she'd marry a future alcoholic with a broken spirit and a reluctance to engage with his children and his wife.

Once married, like thousands of New Yorkers in the 1950s, my parents fled crowded New York City to give their growing families a "better life" in the suburbs: fresh air to breathe, green grass to mow, bushes to be pruned, leaves to be raked, fewer people, and birds chirping instead of police and ambulance sirens blaring. They relocated to New Jersey and, once settled in the Garden State, moved from town to town. Then they moved to Puerto Rico twice in seven years and back to New Jersey, where they settled for two decades. My mom said they relocated sixteen times in twenty years. When she told me that, I asked if my dad had mob ties and was in the witness protection program.

She said no.

My poor mother was a tenacious New Yorker who was uprooted from her beloved Big Apple to live in New Jersey. Then, she lived on an island in the Caribbean where she knew no one and did not speak the language. Talk about culture shock. And she thought the move from New York to Jersey was challenging. A loyal woman, she went with my father and two oldest siblings because she supported my dad's computer business endeavors on the island—twice.

It was living in Puerto Rico the first time where my mother encountered what she believed to be space aliens on the white beach near their home. Upon sighting them, my mother shrieked and ran back home as fast as she could. Knowing limited Spanish, she called the police, who arrived a few minutes later to investigate the odd report. Still frightened and clinging to the cop, my mother walked down to the beach and pointed out to the officer the alien space invaders scuttling about on the white sand. The police officer laughed and, with a chuckle, told her they were *cangrejos herradura gigantes*. She did not understand. Then, in his best broken English, he said they were giant horseshoe crabs—not space aliens.

I know, I know. My mother had a college degree but didn't know what a horseshoe crab was? You have a point. Allow me to defend her, though.

First off, she was a city girl, a New Yorker. My mom knew which subway would take you from Hell's Kitchen to the Bronx or The Battery, what play was appearing at each of the Broadway theaters at any given time, who played centerfield for the Yankees, Dodgers, and Giants, and where to get the best corned beef and cabbage in Manhattan. But sea creatures? Where would she have seen such crustaceans walking around on the streets of New York? In fairness to my mother, her time living in Puerto Rico was during the height of U.S. space exploration and worldwide interest in outer space—the 1950s. TV shows, movies, and radio stations constantly talked about Martians landing on Earth. Mass hysteria about space aliens was sweeping the nation at the time. So it made perfect sense to her. Giant strange-looking creatures she'd never seen before walking around. Of course they were aliens from outer space! What else could they possibly be?

After my father's second stint in Puerto Rico to get his computer business off the ground, he ultimately failed. Again. While bright-minded and educated, my dad was an unsavvy businessman. As such, my parents moved back to New Jersey, settling in Central Jersey's Monmouth County. They bought a 1,400 square foot, four bedroom, two bath Hovnanian home in a new development on a half-acre, premium corner lot. They paid $19,000. Can you imagine that? *$19,000!* Nowadays, that same price would get you a storage shed at Home Depot or a car slightly larger than a grocery shopping cart.

My mother boasted that an aerial photograph of our development showed our property had the most trees in the 300+ home community that sat off Route Nine, an arterial highway memorialized in Bruce Springsteen's "Born to Run" that spanned the length of eastern New Jersey. When she could, my mother worked that little factoid into a conversation, just like I do now.

Each weekday, my father walked three blocks to Jenkins Corner to catch a bus into midtown Manhattan to his job writing computer codes for a midsize company. While my father worked for pay outside the home, my mother worked tirelessly without pay inside it as a stay-at-home mom. She ushered her children to where they needed to be, maintained a spotless house and a well-stocked refrigerator, and operated as the family's chief problem solver.

The year after my family moved back to New Jersey and two weeks after President Kennedy was assassinated, I made my entry into the world. I was an unspectacular-looking future moron with blue eyes and a large cranium that no doubt had some pebbles inside it. No wonder my sister didn't want to look at me for the first month of my life. Who could blame her?

Unlike my oldest brother, Brother 1, who grandly claims he can recall experiences in utero, I can only remember one thing from birth to age three: sitting and playing with my Fisher Price Pound and Saw bench when I was a baby. The little bench had holes in the top and came with pegs, a wooden saw with no teeth, and a plastic hammer. The multi-colored pegs were wood, as was the hammer's handle. I still have that hammer, by the way—some 53 years later. It has a sky-blue handle and a bright yellow plastic head that's pretty roughed up. I'd spend as much time as I could pounding those pegs into the holes before my mom scooped me up from the floor and placed me in my high chair or playpen.

Mom said when I was two, she tried to wean me off baby food and transition me onto regular food, yet I resisted the bird-size portions. As a result, I was still eating baby food at three-and-a-half. I was walking and talking and . . . eating baby food, which was not food at all back then. It was pureed sugar in a glass jar. It was like handing me a Rubik's Cube-size sugar block to gum and swallow. When I was nearly four, my mother put her foot down and transitioned me to regular food, albeit grilled cheese sandwiches, plain American cheese sandwiches on white bread, and tomato soup. These have been a staple of my diet for the last fifty-plus years.

I spent a lot of time in my playpen with my first friend, Michael Michaels. He lived one house away and obviously had parents with a sense of humor. Michael's mother used to bring her cherubic-looking son with golden blond hair cut in a Buster Brown style over to my home, plop him in my playpen, and sit beside my mother on classic blue and white striped webbed folding lawn chairs. As Michael and I pawed at one another in the playpen, our busybody moms spent hours chatting with each other while chain-smoking cigarettes. It was the mid-1960s. That's what adults did back then; they smoked like chimneys. Michael and I became best friends and were inseparable for the next ten years.

When I was three, my mother enrolled me in Mrs. Caruthers' nursery school across the street. It wasn't an official nursery school but a house where working moms dropped off their kids for 3-hours a day to be educated and entertained up to five days a week. By doing so, these mothers could catch a breather, have some Me Time, or work part-time. That unofficial nursery school was my favorite of all the schools I attended. Mrs. Caruthers was a friend of my mom's and was terrific with children. The woman was an angel. She had eight or nine neighborhood kids in her group every weekday. We finger-painted, made arts and crafts, and learned about animals, people, life, and ourselves. That little financially lucrative operation of hers lasted about twenty years before government officials shut it down. It competed with the new corporate preschools and nursery schools built to serve the rapidly growing community. And it was not taxed.

Eventually, weaned off baby food, I developed a finicky appetite with an unbridled urge for cookies, cheese, bread, and milk. While my adolescent friends ate normal foods for breakfast (oatmeal, eggs, bacon, toast, cereal, et cetera), lunch (lunch meat sandwiches, hot dogs, hamburgers, salad, chicken, fish sticks, et cetera), and dinner (fish, chicken, pasta, pork, beef, et cetera), I "ate" Carnation Instant Breakfast every morning from age five to age eighteen. Seriously. I survived and am still here to talk about it.

I ate yellow American cheese sandwiches on white bread, Lindens chocolate chip cookies, Chef Boyardee canned Beefaroni, or fluffernutter sandwiches for lunch. I thought Marshmallow Fluff was part of the food pyramid. I never ate vegetables, fruit, salad, or seafood. I thought fish were disgusting. While most of my friends ate at least some types of seafood, the only fish I'd eat were Goldfish—the Pepperidge Farm crackers—and Swedish Fish—the red chewy candy. Seafood gave me the willies. I thought shellfish, lobsters, and crabs all looked like giant bugs. They all registered high on my *ick* factor as a kid. And after seeing firsthand the process by which lobsters were prepared—leisurely swimming inside a tank one moment, the next being submerged into boiling water to a torturous death awaiting to be eaten—I was done. It seemed brutal. I never witnessed a cow, chicken, or pig die such an excruciating death. If I had as a child, I'd probably still be eating baby food today. And to me, oysters and clams looked like rocks with phlegm inside. I got spooked by their nasty look and smell. I loved sugar, salt, and dairy, which were my diet staples. Looking back, I'm shocked my teeth didn't fall out of my head and that I didn't suffer a heart attack or a stroke by the time I reached the fourth grade. It was eye-opening to realize everyone else had a normal appetite, yet I was a fussy food freak who became a lifelong kooky eater.

My mom admittedly hated cooking. Yet she was a trooper and prepared a different meal for us almost every night: pot roast, London broil, pork chops, spaghetti and meat sauce, and hamburgers. We'd have Elio's pizza or other frozen TV dinners on Friday nights. That was always a treat. My family ate whatever my mom cooked. Except for me, the food fusspot. I wouldn't touch most of it. I would sneakily feed it to our dog, Sherman. The mutt often sat underneath our dining room table between my bony knees, knowing he'd get 90 percent of whatever was on my plate. It took quite an effort to nonchalantly transfer the food from my dish down to Sherman's mouth without being seen by watchful parental eyes. As you can imagine, in no time, Sherman's weight ballooned. Concerned, my mother took him to the vet. The doctor asked my mom what she fed the dog. My mother told him exactly what she gave Sherman, down to the portion size and times per day, following the vet's suggested instructions. The vet weighed Sherman and claimed he ate much more than she reported. Not long after that vet visit, my father caught me feeding Sherman underneath the table. He punished me by making me stand in the corner of our dining room for two hours, which, to a restless child, seemed like two days. A loyal dog who appreciated my efforts in providing him supplemental meals each night, Sherman slept at my feet the entire time I stood in silence in the corner, staring at where two walls met.

As I grew older, people often questioned my bizarre appetite when I ate at their homes. I let them know I was a picky eater because I was used to having a personal chef make my meals as a child. Parents would raise an eyebrow, assuming I was from a wealthy family. That was until I told them my personal chef's name was Chef Boyardee, and it was his processed slop-in-a-can that I ate. (Sorry, Chef!) The food tasted good, though. I acquired a unique taste for processed food. As an adult, I became chef Mike-ro-Wave, as I eat most meals after being heated in a microwave oven. Aside from cookies, candies, cheese, bread, and milk, I loved consuming carnival food and things from lunch trucks—anywhere other than my home. I kept my poor mother on her toes as a kid, that's for sure.

When I was six, I pestered my mother to take me into Manhattan to see the Ringling Bros. and Barnum & Bailey Circus, a rigmarole for any parent to have to schlep her little one into an overcrowded, filthy, and dangerous city, and then back home again. But after I relentlessly wore her down over the weeks, she finally gave in. I was going to the circus to see the elephants, lions, clowns, acrobats, and magicians! I could not wait. Once settled in my seat, I fell asleep. Just like that. And I remained asleep during the entire two-hour circus and on the hour bus ride home. My mom was livid. The next day, I had the gall to ask her if we could return to the Big Top because I had missed all the action. My mother shot me a look, suggesting I never ask that question again. Typical childhood antics that likely put gray hairs on parents' heads and drove some fathers to drink.

One of my favorite childhood memories was traveling by bus from our suburban home in Geneva into Manhattan to pay my mother's parents a visit in their small Upper West Side apartment. We did this once a week during the summer of my sixth year. I remember my mother purchasing the tickets at The Pantry—a local market just outside our development—and then buying me Candy Dots to keep me quiet on the bus. They were small rounded pegs of colored sugar dots attached to a two-foot-long strip of two-inch wide wax paper. If my mouth was busy ripping those tantalizing treats from the wax paper and chewing them, it was less likely to spew words. A well-executed plan that worked. I'd gobble them up on the hour ride into the city, staring out the window, my mother sitting next to me. It was just the two of us, and it didn't get any better than that. I'm not sure if it was before or after we spent a few hours with my grandparents, but we'd always visit a Chock-full 'O Nuts while in the city. I'd sidle up to the lunch counter, climb on a stool beside my mom, and order a vanilla shake, a bowl of tomato soup, and a grilled cheese sandwich. It was my favorite meal. Fifty years later, it still is. I'm unsure why, but I've always had a strange affinity for American cheese. It's all about the simple pleasures in life, right? I sit here now, my eyes watering as I remember those days. My mother is long gone, but the memories of those magical moments are fresh in my mind. I miss her.

D

At age six, I developed severe asthma, sometimes needing to be hospitalized as a result of it. Did you ever have asthma? It sucks. Especially having it as a child when other kids are processing the data you provide them so they can assign you to a particular category for the rest of your youth: athlete, troublemaker, sissy, weirdo, popular, smart kid, fat kid, sick kid, crazy kid, dork, loser, and so on. Asthma is like trying to breathe through a cocktail straw while a 50-lb bag of concrete mix sits atop your chest. Wheezing, it was called back then. My mother took me to my pediatrician for help. As I was wheezing in the examining room, sitting atop the table being tended to by my doctor, my skinny legs dangling from the table like two strands of spaghetti, my mother and my doctor were smoking cigarettes in the small enclosed space. Scratching his head, Dr. Lopez inquired if we had any animals in the house before exhaling a blast of smoke in my face. My mother replied, just our mutt Sherman, following up with her own jet spurt of smoke onto my face. Funny, no one ever asked me if I was allergic to cigarette smoke.

My father offered no help with my health matter despite his having a medical background. I got skewered by him for wheezing. My dad claimed it was all psychosomatic—

which I had to look up in our dictionary—and was convinced I could breathe better if I just put my mind to it. But I put my mind to it. And I still couldn't breathe better. I still had asthma. And it was bad. Real bad. Though I'm no medical doctor, nor have I ever played one on TV, I'm pretty sure the constant clouds of suffocating cigarette smoke levitating around our home and yellowing our walls did not help my condition. My parents collectively smoked three packs of cigarettes a day. While other kids' first words were ma-ma or da-da, my first words were, *Mom, can you buy me more Primatene Mist, please*?

I was a strange boy, stranger than most. I could have been the poster child for weird kids. Aside from my weirdness, I was a skinny boy built like a javelin. Neighborhood dogs often ran up to me and clamped their mouths onto one of my pencil-thin legs to try and bury the slender limb in my backyard, mistaking it for a bone. I'd constantly have to shake them off me.

Not all was bad, though. On the good side, I inherited my father's athletic gene, like my two older brothers. They were sports prodigies in basketball, football, baseball, and track, so I had large shoes to fill. My sister, well . . . I didn't know her. As a kid, I sometimes called the police to report an intruder in the house. The cops would show up and, after investigating, let me know it was my sister. I'd then introduce myself and ask her name. When I was seven and she was nineteen, she married some antisocial, controlling guy much older than her and had a baby, and I saw her even less.

At an early age, I got the memo that my dad didn't want anything to do with me. I was radioactive, toxic. At first, I was incredibly hurt. Like most boys, I longed for my dad's attention, affection, and approval, especially when my friends would tell grand stories of cherished times they spent with their fathers and how their dads taught them this, showed them that, or took them here or there. But I eventually accepted the situation and learned to roll with the punches. Life gives you lemons; you make lemonade. I became a master lemonade maker. I also seemed toxic to my oldest brother, Brother 1, ten years my senior. He avoided me as if I had a deadly plague. I can't entirely blame him, though. How many seventeen-year-olds want to pal around with their seven-year-old kid brothers? Yeah, none is correct. And once my other older brother, Brother 2—the model—three years my senior—became interested in girls, he had little use for me. I was done. Fortunately for him, but unfortunately for me, that happened when he was eleven and I was eight.

    I remember my mother receiving a phone call from a nun at our Catholic school, reporting Brother 2 was caught making out with an eighth-grade girl in the back of the school bus when he was in the fifth grade. Can you imagine that? *Fifth grade!* I didn't have my first awkward kiss until I was in eighth grade. And there was my brother, sucking face like a pro and feeling up some buxom upper-class girl on a Catholic school bus when he was only eleven. He was then, and for many years later, a magnet to females. All the girls swooned over Brother 2. Though I wasn't close with Brother 2 as a kid—and became even more distant when he was a teen and his hormones kicked into overdrive—we occasionally shared some good moments running around the house or outside in our yard, playing sports and army, building forts, and competing as a unified team against other kids in our development in various sports and challenges. Those were times when I experienced fleeting glimpses of him being a good big brother to me. The best example was when I was ten and he was thirteen.

    It was Halloween, and I was trick-or-treating in my neighborhood with my best friend, Michael Michaels. An older boy named Leonard Atkins, whom everyone knew to be bad news was harassing youngsters in costumes as they walked by his house. When I quickly shuffled past Leonard with my head down, doing my best to go unnoticed, he snatched my shopping bag filled with candy treats from my hand. Leonard defiantly stood tall before me and dared me to get it back. I tried, but he easily pushed me down to the ground. He was a stocky fourteen-year-old; I was a ten-year-old who looked like a fetus. I begged and then screamed for him to give me my bag back. He did not. Both Michael's and my efforts to get my shopping bag returned failed.

Defeated, humiliated, and frustrated, I sprinted home with Michael at my side. Upon entering Brother 2's bedroom, I spotted Brother 2 lying on his bed with headphones on, listening to the *Dark Side of the Moon* album by Pink Floyd. Eyes closed and hands folded across his chest, he was entranced in the music when I tapped him on his shoulder. Startled, he noticed tears in my eyes and that I had news to report. When I finished, his demeanor changed. He ripped off the headphones, sprung up from the bed, and ordered me to follow him. Without a word spoken, Michael and I did.

I grew taller and more empowered with each step we took toward Leonard's house. Two blocks later, Brother 2 spotted Leonard sitting on his front porch eating my candy from my shopping bag! My brother approached him and, in one fell swoop, grabbed the bag from the bully's hands and handed it to me. Then he socked Leonard in the nose with his left fist. Leonard fell back onto his porch. My brother stood over him, wagging his finger in Leonard's face, warning the next time he did anything to me, he would get his ass kicked.

Leonard said nothing. His eyes large, he nodded in agreement. Like most people in our development, Leonard knew of Brother 2 and his athletic accomplishments. My older brother was a physical specimen and not one to mess with. At that moment, he was my hero.

Chins up and chests puffed out, Michael and I trailed Brother 2 back home as if ducklings following our mother. Without my brother noticing, I turned around and, with a smirk on my freckled face, gave Leonard the finger. In response, he placed his head down.

That's the power of an older brother.

Getting back my Halloween candy was the nicest thing Brother 2 has ever done for me. I'm not sure if that's a good or a bad thing.

D

Like most kids, I was curious and asked a lot of questions. Unlike the high and mighty priests and nuns at my Catholic grammar school, my mom was the only one to answer them. One day, when I was about nine, I was shopping with my mother at McCrory's Five and Dime in nearby Freehold. Out of the blue, I quizzed my mother why there were official holidays for Mother's Day and Father's Day, but there was no holiday celebrating Children's Day. My mother stopped dead in her tracks and looked me straight in the eye. Through gritted teeth, she snapped, "Every day is children's day, Michael!" It took decades for me to understand what she meant. But she was right.

And like most kids, I endured my share of teasing by bullies.

Alex Piotrowski lived one house away and was my age, though we never became friends. Unlike me, Alex was a sturdily built boy who used his size to intimidate and hector other boys. I was one of the unfortunate few he'd chosen to bully. It was awful. Since I couldn't beat up Alex, to defend myself, I developed a sharp tongue and fought back with words. When Alex taunted me about how skinny I was or teased that I had a Speed Racer lunch box or anything else while standing at the school bus stop, I'd come back with a line attacking him.

"Yeah, I'm skinny, but look at the big gap between your two front teeth! Who parted those teeth, Moses?"

The surrounding kids would chuckle under their breath. Alex would look around to see them stifling their laughs. Then he'd punch me in the chest or push me down, smiling snarkily afterward. If he cracked on me again, I'd come back with another jab at his appearance.

"Look at the size of your head! It's gigantic! It belongs on Easter Island."

The kids would giggle, and Alex would grow more frustrated and punch or push me down again. I'd return to my feet, ready for the next round.

One day, I'd had enough of him targeting me, but I didn't know how to stop him. I asked my mother how best to handle this situation. My mother thought for a few moments and then provided a most unexpected answer. "Tomorrow morning, when you're standing at the bus stop, as soon as that nasty boy approaches you, you hit him right in his fat face with your lunch box."

My eyes widened, and my mouth jutted open upon hearing her advice. I couldn't believe it and had to process what she'd said. *Did my mother just tell me to smash a kid in the face with my metal Speed Racer lunchbox? Awesome!*

I could barely sleep that night, growing anxious about what I would do the following morning.

Sure enough, the next day, as kids were assembled on the corner waiting for the bus, Alex approached me. Before Alex could say a word, I swung my lunch box as if swinging a baseball bat one-handed. Fortunately, I had good hand-eye coordination because that lunchbox landed directly on his fat face, as instructed. The metal box flung open, and out flew my Speed Racer thermos, my cheese sandwich on white bread, and my individual-size bag of Fritos corn chips.

Alex stood dazed for a moment. The surrounding kids watched in disbelief. With blood trickling out both nostrils, Alex grabbed his bleeding nose and shouted, "I can't believe you did this!" over and over before running back to his house. You could hear a pin drop among the assembled crowd of kids. A few minutes later, the large yellow school bus slowly pulled up to the corner, its breaks squeaking as it stopped. I scrambled to retrieve my fallen things scattered about on the ground, quickly jammed them into my newly dented and un-lockable lunchbox, and climbed aboard the bus. Whispers were spoken, and heads occasionally turned to look at me during the thirty-five-minute ride to school. I quietly sat in my seat, not saying a word. At first, I thought about all the trouble I had just gotten myself into. Then I realized I was king of my world for the moment. I slayed the beast.

My mother later reported that a few minutes after the bus took off, there was a loud banging at our front door. My mom opened it to see Alex standing with his head tilted back, holding a bloodied white washcloth to his nose and his mother beside him with fury in her eyes.

"LOOK WHAT YOUR SON DID TO MY SON'S NOSE!" she shouted.

My mom fired back that Alex got what he deserved since he'd been picking on me for weeks, and if she and her son didn't get off her property, my mother would give her a matching bloody nose. Way to go, mom!

I know it's cliché, but that day changed my life. Not only was I never picked on again by Alex Piotrowski, but my stock elevated to new heights among the neighborhood kids and in my Catholic school in another town. That began my reputation as someone who was not playing with a full deck.

Fast forward thirty-plus years.

While strolling in my hometown mall, I thought I spied Alex Piotrowski. Upon passing one another, we both did a double-take look after our eyes met. A flicker of recognition flashed across his face.

After reintroductions and exchanging pleasantries, we briefly talked about the old neighborhood and where our lives had brought us to that point. During our chat, his wife stood beside him with her head down, chewing gum and staring at her cell phone. Alex tapped her on the shoulder and declared, "This is the guy who smashed me in the face with his lunchbox when we were kids. *Remember?*"

Alex's wife lifted her head for the first time, and her face came to life. "Oh, yeah," she crowed. "Now I know who he is."

CHAPTER 2

Freckle-faced Little Devil

Aside from my three siblings, who hadn't the slightest interest in me, my father also made it known that he wasn't interested in spending time with me. I was the only eight-year-old Cub Scout to attend the father-son banquet dinner with *my mother*, acting as a stand-in, yet I had a living father at home. My dad couldn't make that special dinner. He was busy drinking. But my dad and I did go fishing once when I was fourteen and in eighth grade. That's only because my mother forced him to take me as an apology for strangling me one night when he was drunk. Does that count? I'm not sure. I remember the incident like it was yesterday.

After hanging out at my new girlfriend's home—we'd been dating only a few days—I stood with the beauty on her front porch, waiting for my father to pick me up at the designated time. As usual, he had been at the American Legion a few miles away. I observed my family's 1973 blue Pontiac Lemans driving in slow motion up and down the street, passing the house, then turning around and passing it again. I was mortified.

Finally, the car crept up my girlfriend's driveway, halfway on the driveway and halfway on her front lawn. I wanted to disappear into thin air. *Poof!* My dad struggled to exit the car. Once out, he walked unsteadily like a newborn deer. Clutching my girlfriend's hand a bit tighter, I watched with a sense of gathering fear. He stumbled up the porch steps, reeking of cigarettes and beer. I was embarrassed beyond belief. Just when I was about to introduce him to my new girlfriend, my father grabbed me by my neck with both hands and began choking me. Mumbling something unintelligible, he was slurring his words. I gasped for air as he dragged me down the steps and back to the car like I was a wounded gazelle and he was a hungry lion, the white toe tips of my black Converse hi-top sneakers scraping the ground. He was too strong and angry to fight off, though I tried, doing my best to act cool and composed in front of my girlfriend. That was impossible to accomplish in that situation.

Watching in horror, Domonique cupped her hands over her nose and mouth. I wanted to die right then and there. My dad made me look like a fool in front of her. He had long fingers and kept his fingernails unclipped. I felt them good and tight around my skinny neck that night.

The five-minute ride home, I cried in that trying-to-catch-my-breath-between-convulsions way, frightened and not saying a word, realizing I was locked in a car with a drunk man driving—my father. I was reminded of just how dark life can be. Some dads didn't love their sons. And my dad was one of them.

Halfway into the ride, he turned on the radio, which was rare. He preferred silence. The song "I Like Dreamin'" by Kenny Nolan was playing. Details like this are embedded in my brain. Every time I hear that song, I think of that unfortunate moment. I could be sitting on a white sandy beach in the Caribbean, drinking a Margarita and watching a spectacular sunset, or in a canoe in the sparkling blue waters of Lake Louise surrounded by the majestic Canadian Rockies; it wouldn't matter. If that song's played, I'm transported back to that awful moment.

When we pulled up the driveway to our home, I unlocked the passenger side door and leaped out of the car before my father could maneuver the automatic transmission column shifter into park. I bolted into the house past my mom, who noticed me crying. With great concern, she followed me into my bedroom to investigate. I pointed to the scratches on my neck and, as best I could, in between cries, hiccups, and great gulps of air in my hysterical state, gave her the abridged version of events.

Outraged, my mother left my bedroom and stormed over to my father, landing into him. I darted past my parents' arguing, out the front door, and hopped on my Huffy Thunder Road model bicycle. I peddled fast and furiously in the moonlit night, not knowing where to go. The best option I could come up with was my sister's home in Freehold, some six miles away.

Recently divorced and living with her new boyfriend, after reintroducing myself to my sister, she welcomed me inside and allowed me to sleep in her home that night. The next day, my mother informed me that my father said he was sorry (he wasn't) and that he'd like to make it up to me (he didn't) by taking me fishing. For some reason, I agreed to go. Not sure why. I don't even like fishing. Maybe it was so I could tell my own father-son story to my friends, one that didn't involve my dad being drunk and angry and lashing out at me.

Out on the water, I thought that my dad was going to club me over the head with his wooden oar and then dump my body overboard. I could picture him saying, *Don't need this odd one. I already have three other ones.*

During that day in the rowboat in Sandy Hook Bay, I sat facing my father the entire time, never turning my back to him once. I kept thinking *What the hell am I doing here? With him?* Though barely a word was spoken between us, I made it home, unclubbed.

When my dad wasn't being mean, he was ignoring me. It was either one or the other. There was no in-between.

On the flip side, my mother was an angel and the only family member who liked me. While I felt like I had to tiptoe around my house as though treading on eggshells because my father acted as if I didn't belong there, my mom accepted and loved me as the kooky boy I was. She indulged me when it came to food and catered to my every weird food whim. She spoiled me. I readily admit, rotten at times. Because the rest of my family wasn't into me, I thought it evened out. Truth be told, I wasn't into them, either. It was like we were strangers who just happened to live in the same house, like a boarding house. We tolerated each other's existence until one of us left the house to go somewhere else for a period of time. It was uncomfortable. I always felt a sense of alienation there.

Realizing the dynamic with my fragmented family, I decided at age eight to create an alternate family comprised of my friends. Any friend who earned my trust became my brother. Eventually, I grew that surrogate brotherhood to include a half-dozen of my closest friends. Those people were the ones with whom I spent my time, lived my life, and from whom I learned. I've maintained friendships/brotherhoods with most of the guys since then. Simultaneously, some of my friends' fathers became my new surrogate dads. I played catch with them, joked around with them, and often tagged along while they spent time with their sons. Those men were towering influences on me, and no words can accurately describe the void they filled in my life at the time. I was visible to them.

D

While I never got into drugs or drank alcohol during my youth, I did get into mischief, pranks, and scams. Those were my things. Mischief occupied a central role in my childhood. I got such an adrenaline rush being mischievous. It turned out I was pretty good at it, especially with my partner in crime, Michael Michaels. We operated on the same wavelength, knew what each other was thinking, and were able to finish one another's sentences. We not only had the same sick sense of humor, but we had each other's backs. Michael and I shared an incredible bond and became little miscreants together. It was like we were twins, just from different mothers.

When I was nine, I found a New Jersey State Police hat. Michael and I thought of how we could make it useful to both of us rather than only one of us being able to wear it. We brainstormed for a while, bouncing ideas off one another before hatching what we believed was a brilliant plan. We'd steal* candy bars at The Pantry and then pose as children of New Jersey State Troopers and sell them for a dollar each, claiming to raise money for the official-sounding yet made-up New Jersey State Police fund.

While one of us distracted the deli owner with bogus questions, the other would stuff candy bars in his pants and casually slip out of the store. We'd put the looted six or eight candy bars inside the New Jersey State Police hat and then walk to the far side of our development where people were sure not to recognize us. We would then knock on doors to finagle people out of money using false names.

"Hi, I'm Charlie," I'd begin, "and this is Timmy," pointing my thumb to Michael standing beside me.

We'd pause and smile wide from our innocent-looking freckled faces to disarm our prospects.

"Our dads are New Jersey State Police troopers. Would you care to buy a candy bar for a dollar to help support the New Jersey State Police fund?"

Showing the hat, we'd smile again, looking as wholesome as a cup of milk, as if we stepped out of a Norman Rockwell painting. Unsuspecting good-hearted neighbors bought the act hook, line, and sinker. Although we were two little thieving scammers, we *looked like* angelic kids who politely approached with what seemed like a sensible request. *Who wouldn't want to buy a candy bar from us?*

We'd have our six or eight bucks in hand within a half hour. Then we'd peddle our bikes over to Tony's Pizza at the Grand Union shopping plaza and eat away our proceeds. I'd eat a couple of Sicilian slices, and Michael would always get some type of calzone. We'd wait a few days and then hit The Pantry again before soliciting neighboring sections within our spacious development to sell more candy bars.

When I was not pinching candy bars and selling them to unsuspecting adults, I was in Freehold attending St. Mary's Catholic school, achieving As and being told if I ever committed sins, I'd burn in hell for eternity.

Uh, does stealing candy bars count?

I was an insatiably curious boy with an ardent desire to understand what was going on in the world around me and why things were the way they were. As a result, I had a propensity to ask lots of questions. But I didn't have many people at St. Mary's interested in answering them. While my fellow students would frequently shrink away from asking the nuns questions, I'd often raise my hand in the middle of a class lesson and lob such gems as

- How could Jonah be swallowed by a whale, survive inside it for three days, and live? That's impossible!
- How could Noah live to be 950 years old and Noah's grandfather, Methuselah, live to be 969 years old, considering the average person back then lived to only thirty?
- How could Samson lose his strength just because he got a haircut? I got a haircut yesterday, and I'm still as strong as before my haircut!
- If Adam and Eve were the first people, and they made babies together, were their kids retarded?

Some nuns answered such questions through gritted teeth by commanding me to stand and walk to the front of the classroom. When I did, they'd wallop me on the head in front of my classmates with either an open or closed hand—depending on which nun—and then order me to sit back down, zip my mouth shut, and keep my hands on the desk for the remainder of the class. Pretty harsh, huh?

The public humiliation was far more painful than the actual blows. Sometimes, I'd be told I'd have a special place in hell reserved for me if I kept asking such ridiculous questions.

Don't you love all the warmth and kindness those Catholic schools of yesteryear provided?

Because certain nuns constantly threatened me that I'd be going to hell as a way to keep me in line if I didn't do exactly as they said; it messed with my young mind. Truth be told, it left me shaken. It was a traumatic experience for an imaginative child. *Why couldn't they just settle down?* I wondered. I was a curious boy desperate for positive attention and affirmation; I needed proper guidance, encouragement, love, understanding, and support, not angry hags dressed in black who seemed to despise people, especially the kids they taught and oversaw. Deep down, I hated those nasty nuns. But I admit, I feared the hell out of them as well. I wanted to get back at them for the way they treated me. So I devised a plan to go after the head monster, the school's principal, Sister Regina.

There was a hooligan classmate of mine at St. Mary's named Robert Bennett. He was a rough-hewn character with a checkered past. He'd knock books out of your hands when walking down the hall, trip you, and laugh as you fell to the ground. He did that to many school kids, including a few of my friends. Yet I somehow escaped his attention. The nuns often caught Robert acting out, but he remained unfazed after his punishments. He just continued misbehaving.

One day, I decided to exact revenge on him. In the process, I killed a second bird with the same stone.

During recess, a few dozen students played outside in the school's courtyard, a paved macadam parking lot surrounded on three sides by the school's light brick, two-story buildings. I was in the second-story boy's bathroom while Robert was in a stall doing his business. The large wooden bathroom window was open to the courtyard below, and when I glanced out from the ledge, I spied Sister Regina monitoring the active kids. As usual, she wore a scowl and held a wooden paddle, ensuring students noticed it.

I flashed a sly grin. The scene was set.

While the head nun/principal stood at her post, I quietly unrolled several feet of toilet paper from a stall, balled it up, and dunked it in the toilet bowl. Now, I had a giant spitball the size of a baseball. Before Robert exited his stall, I moseyed over to the window and peeked out to make sure Sister Regina was still there.

She was.

I positioned myself for the best angle and launched the sopping-wet mess at Sister Regina. The giant spitball hit her head, knocking her habit sideways. I gulped, and my eyes grew large at the never-before sight of her semi-exposed skull.

After a quick glimpse, I pulled back from the window. At that moment, Robert emerged from the bathroom stall, oblivious to what I had just done. The timing could not have been better. Suppressing my laughter, I casually told him to check out what was happening in the courtyard, where students were stifling their laughter. Robert stuck his big head outside the open window only to encounter Sister Regina staring back, pointing at him, and demanding he go straight to her office. I slowly slinked out the bathroom door and calmly headed to my next class.

Robert vehemently denied throwing the wet ball of toilet paper, but Sister Regina didn't believe him. He was suspended for a week. That was likely the only bad thing Robert didn't do yet was punished for.

*Years after my brief stint pinching candy bars, I visited The Pantry and handed the owner a $50 bill, saying it was for unpaid merchandise I stole years before as a sticky-fingered kid. Appreciating the gesture, he told me to keep my money. I thanked him, then bought fifty $1 lottery tickets and handed them to him.

We were a unique family, that's for sure. Our home was the only one out of the thousands of homes in our town to have a half-court basketball court built on our side property. Can you believe that? My father, brothers, neighbors, and I pitched in to create it when I was eight. It was made of wood, like the pro courts. But when it began to rot a year later due to the elements, we tore it up and replaced it with poured concrete. The backboard and rim faced the sidewalk, inviting passersby to play, which they did. I often found kids—including strangers—on my property, shooting baskets on my court throughout the day. I'd join them, and in no time, other kids would appear, and a competitive game would break out. Throughout my youth, I enjoyed that basketball court every day it did not rain.

Many years later, when my wife and I visited my childhood home every ten years to retrace my footsteps in the old development, I'd see that giant slab of concrete still there, its light blue stain fading over the decades. I'd stare at the slab, conjuring up fond memories. While the pole, backboard, rim, and cotton net are long gone, the surface on which I spent thousands of hours of my youth remains. Over the years, the homeowners have kept it, which makes me smile.

I told you about our basketball court on the side of our property, but did I mention that we also had an old 40-foot wooden Chris Craft boat in our backyard propped up on cinderblocks, built in the 1950s, that didn't float? Well, we did.

My father acquired it from a drinking buddy at the local American Legion post. Maybe he won a bet. Or we lost one. We never really knew. However he got it, we got it. Right smack in the middle of our smallish backyard. For a few years, family, friends, and neighbors pitched in to refurbish it and bring it back to its original glory: sanding it, cleaning it, repairing it, fiberglassing it, and painting it. Curious friends and neighbors alike would occasionally stop over to glimpse the anomaly, asking if we were going to round up two of every creature in our neighborhood once we made the vessel sea-worthy. After four years of that eyesore on our property, my mother demanded that the ark be removed from our backyard.

It was.

The same folks who previously helped repair it pitched in to dismantle it piece by piece. We threw it out for Spring cleanup. Can you imagine that? For the annual garbage pickup, our normal neighbors placed the usual cardboard boxes filled with junk onto the curb, a leaf bag or two, and maybe an old loveseat or recliner. We put out Noah's ark. With zoning laws these days, neighborhood residents call township officials on each other if an American flag or a tiny lawn gnome is put out on a yard without authorization. Our poor neighbors had to deal with a family with a giant boat in our backyard and a basketball court in the side yard. And my parents were among the few college educated parents in our development. Go figure.

In the 21st century, it's all about video games for boys. Morning, noon, night, and moments in between, boys stare at screens and play video games—blowing things up and shooting and killing characters—oblivious to the real world around them. It wasn't that way in my youth. Though we did have video games—including hand-held ones—we enjoyed playing outside in the woods, streets, and parks. What a concept. We were playing *outside*. Imagine that.

Neighborhood pickup games of stickball, baseball, basketball, tackle football, basketball, kick-the-can, ring-and-run, or smear-the-queer. Regarding the latter, if even played at all today, I'm pretty sure the smear-the-queer game is now called smear-the-white-cisgender-heterosexual toxic male. On any day, you'd see packs of kids riding bikes on streets, navigating skateboards on sidewalks, or sledding down neighbors' driveways. The only kids inside their homes were either sick or punished. And they were desperate to come out—their noses pressed against living room or bedroom windows, watching all the action beyond the glass panes—their loving mothers preventing them from leaving the house.

Few things were more exciting during my childhood than venturing into the woods surrounding half my development. We were not just kids but adventurers exploring the unknown wilderness. Entering the woods was like stepping from one world into another, discovering new sights, sounds, and smells. A temporary refuge away from family, school, and life's problems. Our woods had hundreds of acres filled with trees and meadows, small ponds, a stream, animals, and trails—even an old shack with an ancient, overall-wearing ornery farmer living in it. When the farmer knew kids were back on his property, he'd chase after us as fast as his geriatric bones would allow, hollering that we were trespassing. Sometimes, he'd shoot at us with his shotgun filled with salt. That old bastard hated us trespassing kids. I can't blame him, though. We were little pests. His shotgun never kept us away for too long, though. We kept intruding. It was too important a place for us to give up. If we had to take some salt-shot stinging wounds to the body, so be it. Eventually, time caught up with those woods, and they became developed. Trees bulldozed, ponds filled with dirt, and expensive McMansions, Starbucks, banks, Subways, chain-store pharmacies, and more Starbucks replacing them. But when they were there—between my birth and the age of sixteen—they served as a magical getaway and hideaway where our imaginations ran wild. Since some Revolutionary War battles were fought on those same grounds, my friends and I would occasionally find relics such as powder horns (used to hold gunpowder for soldiers), cannon balls, musket balls, leather pouches, Colonial coins, and shreds of clothing. We even found remnants of an old flag with stars on it. Of course, as dopey kids, we didn't know the value of our finds. We would sell or trade those items to other kids in the development, usually older boys who knew their worth and easily took advantage of us.

THEM: I'll give you this new pack of bubble gum for that smelly, old, ripped-up flag you found.

US: Uh . . . OK.

The woods contained a few ponds on which we skated and played hockey in the winter. One we named the peanut pond due to its shape. We built forts and rode our bikes and motorcycles over jumps we'd formed from mounds of dirt. We swung over a narrow creek from the rope swing tied to a large silver maple tree limb. That was my enchanted forest, a holy sanctuary from the chaos and unwelcomeness at home.

Decades later, my wife and I have occasionally revisited my old neighborhood. We'd walk the streets and see not a child in sight. Not one. In my youth, the streets were always packed with kids engaged in various activities while parents and neighbors alike chatted with each other on front lawns, sidewalks, or driveways. Sadly, that's not happening today. Kids and parents today are inside playing video games, texting, or posting to (anti)social media. While some woods are left these days, nobody's exploring or enjoying them. They're eerily empty.

Not all of my experiences in the woods were beautiful memories.

For some reason, when I was eleven, my best friend Michael Michaels and I thought it'd be a good idea to head back into the woods, light the end of a long, thick rope on fire, and then take turns swirling around in circles holding it in our hands.

What can I say? We were morons. (Hence the subtitle of this book)

The surrounding area was set ablaze in no time, and our fun came to a screeching halt. I tried extinguishing the fire by scooping dirt onto the flames as quickly as possible. Despite my efforts, the fire grew larger. Spooked, we looked at each other and made a mad dash out of the woods. Short of breath, we found an older neighbor and asked him to call the police because we saw a fire in the woods. Of course, we left out the part that *we started it*. Within a few minutes, two red fire trucks and one police car zoomed down the street to where we were standing, sirens blaring and horns screeching. Neighbors flew out from their houses and flocked to the scene at the dead end of my street, near the main entrance to the woods. The lone police officer questioned Michael and me about what we witnessed, his hands holding a paper pad and a pen. We concocted a story and told them a yarn about how we glimpsed an older boy carrying a large red can in his hands leaving the woods. The officer's eyebrow raised, wanting to know if it was a gas can. We shrugged and said it looked like one, but we weren't sure what was in it. The officer asked if we knew the older boy and could identify him. Michael and I said we only saw the back of his head, and he had long brown hair and wore cut-off dungarees. We claimed he was about seventeen. Since it was the mid-'70s, that description fit almost every late teen male living in America. Good luck finding him. Because we were only eleven and looked like believable boys, the officers bought our story, and we were free to go. Michael and I swore to never touch another match again for the rest of our lives.

 Not all my childhood activities included mischief and selling pilfered candy bars. One of the productive, non-scam activities in which Michael and I engaged—especially on rainy days—was to write letters to our favorite professional athletes. Sports legends of the day such as Hank Aaron, Willie Mays, Roberto Clemente, Walt Frazier, John Havlicek, Rick Barry, and several others. We bought a sports magazine that listed the addresses of professional football, basketball, and baseball teams. Sitting at the dining room table in my home, we wrote dozens of letters. My mother gave us her writing pad, pens, envelopes, and roll of 8-cent stamps. She was an angel. We'd spend hours hand-writing letters in script to our favorite athletes, letting them know we were their biggest fans . . . and then requesting the sports luminaries send us an autographed picture of themselves. We'd mail to the team's address, c/o the athlete's name. Typically, within a month, we'd receive a response in the mail. We'd excitedly open the envelopes and often pull from them form letters with our requested signed autograph pictures tucked inside. As you can imagine, Michael and I were the happiest kids in town. First, to be considered important enough to receive mail, and then to have those priceless items delivered to us by world-famous professional athletes we looked up to. It didn't get much better than that. I've given most of those autographed pictures away to the children of my family and friends over the years, but I once had an impressive collection of autographed photos of the greatest legends ever to play their sport.

The most cherished autographed picture I received was from my favorite athlete at the time, Pittsburgh Pirates baseball superstar Roberto Clemente. I sent the right fielder a heartfelt letter, letting him know how much I respected and admired him and how much he inspired me as a Little League baseball player. I even told Roberto that my parents had lived in his home country of Puerto Rico twice.

Two weeks after I mailed my letter, while watching TV from my living room, I learned Roberto was killed in a plane crash. I was crushed.

Though Puerto Rican, Roberto was making sure food and supplies would be delivered to the survivors of an earthquake in Nicaragua in late 1972. People donated items and money to the earthquake victims, but the intended recipients did not receive those supplies. Instead, corrupt Nicaraguan government officials stole the donated items and kept them for their own use or sold those donated supplies to the highest bidder.

Knowing his status as a beloved figure in the Latin American community worldwide, Roberto knew those items would reach the intended people if he boarded a plane with food and supplies. So he hopped on a small aircraft in Carolina, Puerto Rico, to complete his humanitarian mission.

Just after take-off on the dark, moonless night of December 31, 1972, the DC-7 carrying Roberto Clemente crashed into the ocean just off the coast near Piñones. The Hall of Famer's body was never recovered. He was thirty-eight. My idol was dead. And I was gutted.

A few weeks after Roberto's tragic and untimely death, I returned home from St. Mary's via the big yellow school bus, slump-shouldered and still in mourning. Busy dusting the living room, my mother greeted me and casually mentioned that I received a letter from the Pittsburgh Pirates. The envelope was on the kitchen table.

Wait—what?

I dropped my schoolbooks, rushed to the orange-painted kitchen, and excitedly yet carefully opened the envelope. I slowly extracted a letter and a signed autograph photo of Roberto Clemente—in his distinctive signature. [*Cue the bright ray of light beaming down on me from the sky with the sound of a choir singing*] I could not believe it. It was a miracle, and I was overcome with emotion. When receiving such treasures, I would lick my right index fingertip and carefully touch that digit upon the end of the signature to determine its status. If the ink smudged, it was personally signed. If it did not smudge, it was a Xerox copy the likes of which some stars sent. Using my tried and true method on Roberto's signature, the ink smudged. It was an authentic signature, not a facsimile. My smile grew wider.

I proudly kept that signed picture of Roberto Clemente for the next four decades before gifting it to former UFC world champion Frankie Edgar to thank Frankie for his humanitarian efforts in helping my disabled students over the years. In doing so, I handed the future UFC Hall of Famer a piece of my heart to pass down to one of his children.

Whenever I see someone wearing a throwback Roberto Clemente jersey or a Pittsburgh Pirates T-shirt with the number 21, I approach them and tell them the story about the special gift I received from Roberto when I was a boy back in January 1973.

Every time I relay that story to strangers, I get chills. And more often than not, the person hearing it tears up.

That's the power of Roberto Clemente. As great a player as Roberto was on the field, he was an even better man off it.

CHAPTER 3

Demons and Priests

Everybody loved Brother 2. He was a kind, polite, and quiet kid who did not possess the mischief genes I somehow received as a child. He was an exceptionally gifted all-around athlete, one of the best in my hometown and the surrounding towns. Boys of all ages wanted to be around him. Even with his good looks and superior athletic talent, Brother 2 was a humble, happy-go-lucky boy who always kept his ego and emotions in check. He had the inner calm of the Buddha.

When he turned twelve, he began hanging around kids who were my oldest brother's age—nineteen. My mother was not thrilled about it and voiced her concerns. Around that time, Brother 2's mood began to change. He'd go from calm one moment to a raging lunatic the next, with incredible strength that took the collective muscle of my father and oldest brother to restrain him when he went berserk. Brother 2's mood swings were scary, unpredictable, and violent.

Nobody in my family had ever witnessed him act like this before. It came out of nowhere and was terrifying. It was like he was possessed. But there he was, acting like a raging maniac several times a week, without warning before his behavior would change.

The year was 1973. *The Exorcist* was playing in movie theaters across America. People talked about the spine-chilling film, especially in my Catholic elementary school.

In the movie, a demon takes possession of a twelve-year-old girl who wreaks havoc upon her upper-class family. Although *The Exorcist* was rated R, my friend Michael and I snuck into a matinee showing as nine-year-olds. As expected, the film scared the bejeezus out of us. After watching *The Exorcist*, I was convinced the devil possessed my brother. Like the girl in the movie possessed by a demon at age twelve, Brother 2 was also twelve. It made perfect sense to me as a nine-year-old Catholic schoolboy.

I did my best to steer clear of Brother 2 during that distressing time, but living in the same house and sharing a bedroom with him made it impossible to hide. I was terrified by the thought of sleeping in the same home as him, let alone the same bedroom. Recognizing the abnormal and dangerous behavior my brother suddenly exhibited, my mother moved him to a downstairs bedroom, away from me. I was relieved. When not outside my home or fearing my brother inside it, I'd read my series of How and Why Wonder books in my bedroom, escaping the elements raging around me.

To find out the cause of Brother 2's bizarre behavior, my mother took him to see a child psychiatrist. After a series of appointments, the shrink determined Brother 2 had a brain tumor, which he reasoned was causing the behavior. Luckily, further tests proved Brother 2 did not have a brain tumor. It turned out he had a lousy child psychiatrist.

To get to the root cause of my brother's inexplicable behavior, my mother committed him to a hospital for psychiatric evaluation. After two weeks of intensively studying Brother 2, the hospital's findings were inconclusive. They kept him heavily drugged during his stay, which made him sleep most of the time and groggy when he was awake. We were back at square one. Concerned family members were left scratching their heads, trying to figure out the cause of my brother's violent episodes. A few months in, I held firm in my belief that a demon possessed him.

It was an absolutely terrifying time in my household. One day, Brother 2 chased me with a long steak knife in his hand and a maniacal look in his eyes, saying in a spine-chilling and unrecognizable voice that was not his own that he was going to kill me. I ran faster than ever to Michael Michaels' house, entered, and locked all the doors. I was shaking, scared out of my wits. I slept there the next few days until matters settled down back home.

It was not until a few weeks after this latest episode when I discovered what appeared to be a cigarette butt in the sleeping quarters of our backyard boat, that my family uncovered the truth. I handed the odd-looking fragment to my mother, who examined it carefully. Both my mom and I knew it didn't look like any cigarette she or my dad had ever smoked. My mother passed the unknown object along to my father, who paid to have it tested at a lab. A few days later, the results were in.

It turned out Brother 2 was smoking marijuana laced with Phencyclidine—PCP—also known as angel dust. It's a drug that causes hallucinations, distorted perceptions of sounds, along with violent behavior.

Bingo!

Brother 2 did the right thing when confronted with the evidence and fessed up. He claimed he received the joints from a classmate at school. The good news was that the root of Brother 2's erratic behavior was identified, and he stopped doing drugs. But I felt he was never quite the same after his six-month drug usage. I'll leave it at that. There was a silver lining in that scary cloud: he still looked like a model!

After witnessing firsthand the adverse effects of my brother's brief drug usage and my father's alcohol consumption, I steered clear of drugs and alcohol in my youth. I didn't need them to make me wacky. I was already a crazy kid with a nutty appetite, to boot.

My poor mother. She had an enormous pile of excrement dumped upon her by her family members: an emotionally distant, sporadically-employed, alcoholic husband; her lone daughter marrying some older, anti-social control freak; her favorite and best-looking child using a psychotropic drug and turning into a madman at times; her oldest son a march-to-the-beat-of-his-own-drum type; and her youngest child a weird, emaciated kid with asthma who didn't eat anything other than a few items of processed garbage. Like most kids, I underappreciated all she did for us.

My mother's actions could've easily qualified her for sainthood. She always drove us active boys to wherever we needed to be: sports games or practices, church events, school affairs, friends' homes, doctors' appointments, movie theaters, anywhere. And she never once complained. She was the best mother up until I was fourteen. Then she did the best she could despite the challenges—that being my father's increasing alcoholism and nightly absenteeism. And she did her best with me considering my limitations as a silly fourteen-year-old hormonal boy.

While I was well-behaved in my home, I had peculiarities and obsessive-compulsive tendencies that were challenging to interpret and understand. I kept my mother scratching her head most of the time. Case in point: I'd wear multiple pairs of thick tube socks to help make my skinny calves and ankles appear thicker.

During back-to-school shopping with my mom one day, we made our annual visit to Al's Bootery in downtown Freehold so I could be fitted for new school shoes. I was ten at the time. I took off one sneaker and placed my one-socked foot inside the metal Brannock device that measures a person's shoe size and width. My foot was a size 14. The shoe salesman remarked how large my foot was for a child. He then requested I remove my sock so he could get a more accurate measurement. I peeled off a sock on my foot, yet that foot was still covered with a sock. The shoe salesman glanced up at my mother, then back at me, and asked me to take off *that* sock. I did. Another sock remained. He scratched his head and looked up at my mother again, claiming he needed my foot to be bare—totally sockless. I peeled off four more pairs of socks, one right after the other—six pairs in total—shrinking my foot to a size 8. My mother stood watching with her arms folded, shaking her head, and gave me the deadeye stare. Bewildered, the salesman questioned why I wore so many socks.

I shrugged and told him I had a lot of socks.

Here's another example of how I must have driven my mother crazy. Before heading outside to wait for the yellow school bus to transport me to St. Mary's, I would have my mom inspect the length of my white shirt sleeves to ensure they were the same length on my wrists. Commonly known today as OCD behavior, four-plus decades ago, it was not understood, classified, or diagnosed. My mother thought my behavior was strange. If one of my sleeves were even a half-inch shorter or longer than the other one, it would throw me off. It would be all I could think about at the moment. Someone could be jabbing knitting needles into my eyeballs, which would be of secondary concern to the lengths of my sleeves. I needed my mom to fix it, which was quickly done with a quick adjustment of the shorter sleeve.

The poor lady.

I never claimed to be a great little brother. I was a little shit like most attention-deprived kids. As payback for not including me in their daily lives, I sometimes used to steal my older brothers' clothes, records, sports cards, magazines, and the like, then set up a folding table on my street corner and sell their possessions to the neighborhood kids milling about on the streets. Also invisible to his two older brothers, Michael stole things from his brothers as well. The stars aligned perfectly, so we joined forces, filling one large table with our older brothers' belongings.

Sitting on folding lawn chairs, Michael and I solicited customers, honed our sales skills, and became wheeler-dealers. We sold everything and pocketed several dollars apiece for only a couple of hours of "work." Of course, we'd get a good clobbering when our older brothers spotted a neighborhood kid wearing their hat or T-shirt or when they couldn't find their favorite sports cards, magazines, or other items.

If they spent time with us as their little brothers, then we wouldn't have sold their shit. That's the way Michael and I saw it.

But I wasn't all bad. I did do some honest work as a lad. Unlike many of today's boys who play video games for most of the non-school day and don't seek employment until their late teens or early twenties, I was entrepreneurial and hustled to earn an honest buck. Starting at age eight, between Thanksgiving and Christmas, I sang Christmas carols door-to-door with Michael or Brother 2 when he was available. We'd get a dollar for singing two or three carols per home. When I was nine, Michael and I began shoveling snow from my neighbors' driveways and walkways. We'd do a handful of homes before becoming exhausted, earning about $20 each in cash for four or five hours' worth of work. At that age, $20 was like a million dollars because it could buy us things we wanted: sports cards, bubble gum, slices of Pizza at Tony's Pizza, and pinball games at The Pantry. It was empowering. When I was ten, I got a paper route delivering the *News Transcript*. Throughout my development, I rode my black Huffy bike and slung papers onto customers' driveways or porches, collecting money and tips every other Friday after school. I proudly held that job for three years, delivering in all kinds of weather. I made a buck however I could, sometimes with honest work, sometimes not.

D

Despite my mother being a hardened New Yorker who didn't pull any punches when speaking her mind, she was a divine being in my life from birth until age fourteen. She catered to my every whim, making me grilled cheese sandwiches when the rest of my family ate food I wouldn't touch. She calmed my childhood OCD by pulling my shirt sleeves to matching lengths before I hopped on the school bus. She drove me to countless places in my youth. She made sure I had clean clothes and was always warm and fed. She tended to my severe asthma fits and scratched my back to help me fall asleep on some nights because my mind was racing, thinking of an assortment of things. Though my Irish mother was not the kind of mother to be demonstrative with hugs, kisses, and spoken I love you's, I felt her love through her tough exterior. She was my lone protector all the time. She was the best. My mother could be my closest ally, but she could also be my harshest critic.

Fast forward.

I recall when I was in my thirties and requested she read my just-completed original screenplay about the legendary curse Babe Ruth put on the Boston Red Sox after they sold him to the New York Yankees in 1919. My film, *Bambino's Curse,* is an uplifting, mythic fantasy that combines historical facts with baseball folklore and is a mixture of "Field of Dreams," "The Natural," and "Ghost." My mother was a Yankees fan who was lucky enough to see The Bambino play at Yankee Stadium when she was a little girl, so I believed she'd enjoy the story. Though the 120-page manuscript should only take about two hours to read, I gave her much more time than that.

Two weeks later, I phoned her and asked what she thought of the hopeful future movie I was shopping around to Hollywood screenwriting agents in hopes of securing representation. My mother reported that she didn't get past page three.

Huh?

I told her she obviously was not an Evelyn Wood speed reading graduate and then asked why she hadn't finished the screenplay. My mom curtly remarked that I misspelled the word "cemetery" on page 3—I spelled it "cemetary," and she couldn't get past that error.

I stood with my mouth open, the phone receiver dangling from my hand. I explained it was just a typo and that spell-check didn't catch the innocent mistake, but it didn't matter to her. She felt I should've known how to spell the word. And if I didn't know how to spell that simple word, *how could I possibly know how to write a screenplay*?

Miffed, I hung up the phone and immediately drove nearly an hour from where I lived in Pennsylvania to her home in New Jersey. I pulled into the short driveway and rang the doorbell of the condo she lived in with my father.

With no awareness, my mother welcomed me with a big smile, remarking what a pleasant surprise it was to see me. I brushed past her into the foyer, asking where my screenplay was. With a bemused expression, she pointed to it, sitting on the dining room table where my father was smoking a cigarette. Without saying a word, I tromped over, fetched the screenplay, acknowledged my father with a nod, and stormed out the front door, where my mother still stood. I entered my car and drove an hour back home to Bucks County.

As you see, my mom was not the kind to heap praise on anything you did, especially if it was not up to her standards. There were no hosannas saluting my work.

While attending St. Mary's from first through fifth grade, I felt like I lived in two different worlds. Although I lived, played, and participated in youth sports programs in my hometown of Geneva, I spent most of my day in school in the neighboring town of Freehold. However, most kids who attended St. Mary's lived in Freehold. Although it was only seven miles from my home, it felt a world away. I had my Freehold school friends and my Geneva school friends, but the two groups never mixed.

If I'd spent a weekend sleeping over my Freehold friend's home, my Geneva friends would become jealous, and vice versa. I spoke a different language than my Freehold friends regarding our athletic endeavors, funny things our buddies did, social happenings, etc.

If my hometown Geneva football team won an exciting game after coming from behind because Drew Collins caught my pass and ran for a 30-yard touchdown to win on the game's final play, and I relayed that story to my Freehold friends, they'd look at me with glazed faces. They had never heard of Drew Collins. And they didn't care about my hometown football league. It was not *their* league. They'd extend me the courtesy of listening to my accounts but only had an interest in what happened in their Freehold football league, how their guy intercepted a pass and ran for a touchdown, and how they scored two touchdowns. There was a breakdown in communication, a disconnect between us. Something had to give. Finally, at the end of fifth grade, I made a pitch to my mother to pull me out of St. Mary's and enroll me in public school for sixth grade so I could attend with my hometown friends.

For a lifelong devout Catholic like my mother, that was considered heresy. She attended Catholic grammar and high school, graduated from a Catholic college, married a fellow Catholic school product, and attended Catholic mass every Sunday. My suggestion of the move was tantamount to requesting we relocate to India and join the Hare Krishnas. But I made my case.

Look at all the money our family would save (St. Mary's was about $800 a year back then). I'd get home earlier each weekday to focus on my homework and chores around the house. And if all that wasn't enough, I added some more reasons. As a disaffected student, I'd had enough of the nuns' cold-hearted meanness, inflexibility, and invading my personal space by smacking me on the head, pulling me by the ear, or rapping my knuckles with a ruler and telling me if I didn't watch myself, I'd be headed straight to hell. I guess you could say they smacked the Jesus out of me. I'd become disillusioned with the whole Catholic school experience and was repelled by the school's hypocrisy and the sisters' fearmongering.

After some cajoling mixed in with badgering, my arguments fell on fertile ground, to my amazement. Thankfully, my mother listened to my impassioned plea and agreed. And so I began sixth grade at Lafayette Mills School in Geneva. It was both refreshing and shocking at the same time.

It was refreshing because I was no longer smacked with open hands, rulers, pointers, paddles, or bibles. And it was shocking because I could not believe how unruly and openly disrespectful kids in public school behaved. And that was 1976—in a middle-class suburban school in a safe town—not in a bad neighborhood or present day where the kids, not the educators, run the classrooms. I also could not believe how lenient the teachers were in my new school.

On my first day of class in public school, a classmate named Eugene Colombo tossed an eraser at the teacher and hit her. The chalk from the impact left a white, rectangular, powdered mark on the back of her dark blouse. The teacher turned around and calmly responded, "Eugene, if you throw one more thing, I'm sending you to the principal's office."

Ten seconds later, with a big dumb grin on his angular face, Eugene threw one more thing. Yet he was not sent to the principal's office, as warned. I was shocked.

If that happened in St. Mary's, the nun would silently walk over to the kid who tossed it, wallop the kid on the head with a forceful blow, grab the kid's ear, twist it, and escort the misbehaved student out of the classroom and down to the principal's office. And that bad boy would get expelled. Bye-bye. Then, a school administrator would swiftly call one of the many families on the long St. Mary's waiting list and tell the mother the fantastic news: there was an opening at St. Mary's, and your son/daughter was next in line. The open spot would be filled within minutes.

In Catholic school, the slightest act brought forth the wrath of the nuns upon children's skulls. Accidentally dropping a book on the floor, fidgeting in your chair, or incorrectly holding a pencil in your hand meant a smack on the head. In public school, kids would disrespectfully talk back to teachers, challenge or threaten them, curse at them, and throw objects at them. And all that bad behavior seemed OK with the teachers and administrators. That was my introduction to the liberal way of handling bad behavior. Do nothing and hope it goes away; place hope over reality. It was mind-boggling to witness. I'd gone from one extreme to the other. It'd be like taking a burka-wearing woman raised in a strict religious environment, putting her in a string bikini, handing her a beer and a blunt, and then having her go live with the *Jersey Shore* cast for the summer. Culture shock.

My new sixth-grade classmate, Eugene, was a piece of work. He was like every Italian kid I knew then. He looked like a grown man: developed muscles, facial hair, a deep voice, one long, uninterrupted eyebrow, and a raging libido—all at age twelve. In contrast, I looked like a freckle-faced fetus whose hormones wouldn't be awakened for a few years.

Eugene wasn't the brightest boy and often acted out in class, disrupting it most days. Both during and after class, he'd hit on the girls. They'd roll their eyes, clutch tightly to their schoolbooks pinned to their budding chests, and stride away. He'd also pick on his male classmates, which eventually included me. It was a rite of passage for most boys, I suppose. Although I had experience dealing with a bully a few years before—the boy I struck in the face with my Speed Racer lunchbox—I wasn't sure slamming anything into Eugene's skull would stop him from picking on me. His head was an anvil the size of a Macy's Thanksgiving Day Parade float. It would have probably made him madder.

Day after day, Eugene's unwanted attention toward me escalated, and I became the sole focus of his bullying. I could no longer handle it. Responding to him with my defensive wisecracks only made him punch me harder and brought more unwanted attention to me. As the new kid in a new school, this was not good. Fortunately for me, at the time, I was watching the *Rich Man, Poor Man* miniseries on TV. It inspired me.

Nick Nolte's character, Tom Jordache, fought back against his nemesis, a tough guy character named Falconetti, played by the bodybuilding actor William Smith. If average-built Tom Jordache could fight back against Falconetti—a muscled Italian, like Eugene—then I could fight back against Eugene. So, I came up with a plan to stand up to him.

The night before I was to confront Eugene, I could not sleep. Images of me getting pummeled in the school hallway while my new public school classmates looked on in horror terrified me. I'd have to change schools. The following morning, I was as ready as I could ever be. I have never been more nervous, before or since, in life.

Standing outside homeroom, I spotted Eugene strolling down the hallway, knocking one kid's hat off his head, slapping another kid's books out of his hand, making a fist and motioning to punch someone else, and pulling back and snickering/ Then his eyes landed squarely on me. When they did, a wave of panic rushed over me.

I stood for a moment before I could gain command of my thoughts. Then, gradually, with each step Eugene took my way, my fright increased. As he approached to intimidate me, he removed his T-shirt. His bulging muscles of his broad physique knotted as he stepped closer. I swallowed some built-up saliva and wondered what I'd gotten myself into. We circled each other like animals, sizing up one another, before Eugene stepped closer to me and commented about how skinny I was. I zoned out on what he'd said and, instead, silently rehearsed the words I'd practiced for hours the previous evening. The crowd slowly closed in around us, forming a circle.

Reciting from the script I memorized the night before, I let Eugene know I wasn't going to take his shit anymore, and I was willing to fight him after school. The crowd gasped.

I acknowledged that he'd kick my ass, but I wasn't afraid of him, and I'd at least get a few shots in.

Eugene inched closer, making our noses touch. He narrowed his dark brown eyes and kept his steely gaze on me. I could smell his breath and morning meal. A banana, if you're wondering. Underneath my facade of confidence, I was trembling inside and did my best to mask my fear. That few seconds it took for Eugene to process what I'd said while we stared eye-to-eye with each other felt like forever. Without taking my unblinking eyes off him, I tried to see if his hands were clenching or moving to be able to avoid a strike. A few boys in the background roared *Hit 'em*, goading us to engage. I was stunned when Eugene's scowl slowly broke into a broad smile. The muscled man-child shoulder-clapped me and said we were cool and he didn't fight his friends.

For the first time in a long fifteen seconds, I exhaled. Crisis, bloody nose, bruised ego, and humiliation in front of my new schoolmates were all averted. Eugene decided he wanted to be my friend. And he was, never picking on me again for the remainder of sixth grade.

A few years later, in high school, I questioned Eugene Columbo why he didn't pulverize me back then, which he easily could have done. He chuckled, claimed he liked me, and respected that I stood up to him. Eugene told me I was one of the few kids who ever had.

Within the first few weeks of entering public school in the sixth grade, a girl in my grade named Heather Brown began to take notice of me in class. She'd often turn around in her front-row seat, smile, and write me notes. They'd say things such as *Hello!* or *I like your smile*, and they'd be folded several times and passed down the aisle to me, seated in the middle of the row. Or she'd slip them in my hand after class when I walked down the hallway en route to my next class. Heather's actions were quite confusing to me. I knew the girl because her dad was an assistant coach on my youth football team, and she was one of the cheerleaders for the team. But I never gave her a second thought. My hormones were not yet active. I didn't know how to respond to all the unwanted attention she heaped on me, so I didn't respond. But that didn't stop more smiles and notes from coming.

In mid-February, Heather handed me cards and little pastel-colored Valentine's Day mints with written sayings. (*You're cute, Be My Valentine*) She even invited me to her house and the movies. *What was going on here?*

I was twelve, hung out with my guy friends, and only went to the movies with my buddies. Why would I ever want to see a movie with a girl? I was repulsed at the thought and had zero interest in spending time with girls, even if it was the perky and pretty Heather Brown.

Fast forward three years.

Guess who was one of the best-looking freshman girls in high school whom most boys—including the juniors and seniors—wanted to date?

Heather Brown.

In contrast to Heather's physical beauty as a high school freshman, I was an absolute mess, thanks to puberty. I resembled an abstract painting: distorted face, zits the size of the Grand Tetons covering my oily face; braces like train tracks covering my teeth; bushy eyebrows that each resembled a Tom Selleck mustache and a voice pitched so high it made Mickey Mouse sound like country singer Trace Adkins. To boot, I looked like a skeleton.

When I tried to cash in my Heather Brown-once-liked-me-chips from sixth grade and asked Heather as a freshman in high school if she'd like to hang out sometime—perhaps go to a movie?—Heather's face scrunched as if a skunk had sprayed her. She put her hand on her shapely cheerleader's hip, rolled her green eyes, and exhaled. "As if!" she exclaimed and sashayed away, her gaggle of minions trailing her like ducklings.

Oh, well. I tried.

As mentioned, I was mostly an A student until the seventh grade. However, I began having difficulty processing what I'd read in eighth grade. I could read the words fine; I just couldn't *understand* what I'd read. Then I'd have to read everything a second and third time, breaking the paragraphs into smaller parts: a single word, a sentence, two sentences. It felt weird and was a great source of shame for me. *Was I dumb*? I didn't think I was dumb. For the first time in my life, I struggled to comprehend what I'd read. Those SRA multi-colored reading cards were a nightmare, and I couldn't advance beyond the lowest color levels. I approached my mom about the problem, but she advised me to pay better attention in class. My dad, well, he didn't care—no need to approach him. He'd only become angrier at me.

Feeling like a dunce and quickly realizing academics would not be my key to happiness and success, I began acting out. While some kids in my situation would have taken the bully route or the drugs and alcohol route to dull the shame I felt, I chose the mischievous clown route. As a result, my athletic performance suffered.

Although I was a good athlete, I knew I would never be the best athlete in my school. By eighth grade, kids had grown taller, broader, and heavier than me. Simply put, they had developed more quickly. I didn't know it then, but I would become a late bloomer, not fully developing physically until I was twenty. Since I wasn't going to be the best athlete in school and I certainly wasn't going to be the best student in school, I strived to be the best and craziest clown in school. Make people laugh, even at my own expense. That would get me attention from my peers and divert attention away from my academic deficits. As a kid struggling with a myriad of issues, it was all about deflection and acting out. The bully beats up kids in school because he's getting beat up at home. The class clown acts out with crazy antics so his peers don't notice he's struggling with his reading comprehension issues. So, that was the path I chose at that time in my life.

Mandy Evans was my age and lived a few blocks away. Her older sister married my best friend Michael's oldest brother, which is how I came to know her. The girl was a knockout.

Despite only being thirteen, Mandy was one of those females who developed early. She had enormous breasts, a thin waist, and a large, rounded posterior—like two basketballs placed beside each other. Girls her age didn't look like *that*. Boys and girls alike often turned their heads to glimpse her when she walked by. Mandy could have easily passed for a college student. That curvaceous figure roused new feelings in my own undeveloped thirteen-year-old body. My synapses began firing.

When I first stumbled upon Mandy, it was at Michael Michaels's home. Having no game, I had no idea what to say to her. I just gawked at the girl as she bounced around in her bikini in Michael's above-ground pool while snapping Bubble Yum bubble gum inside her pretty mouth. When my gawking approach didn't grab her attention, I tried to stand out by throwing a football with Michael in the street in front of her house as she practiced doing cartwheels on the front lawn with a gaggle of boys buzzing around her. As a youth football quarterback, I tossed a pigskin with accuracy and a tight spiral. Coaches said I was a natural. In my backyard, I used to tie a car tire to a tree limb via a rope. I'd have friends push the tire back and forth while I stood five or ten yards away, throwing footballs through the tire as it swung. So tossing a football to kids running passing patterns was my pathetic go-to move to gain Mandy's attention. The problem was that other boys were also vying for her attention. I had competition. Lots of it. Kids my age to older boys in high school; boys with mustaches doing kickflips on their skateboards; shirtless boys with chiseled pecs and six-pack abs wrestling or slap-fighting each other; and boys doing wheelies on their souped-up bicycles. There was even a kid I'd never seen before riding his unicycle, trying to gain Mandy's attention. Where that boy came from, I had no idea. To everyone's surprise, he just showed up in my development one day. The scene was like a three-ring circus with all the various performances. The only thing missing were the jugglers and the lion tamers. I had to come up with something unique to set myself apart from the crowded field. Fortunately, I had a few screws loose. So, I used that to my advantage and thought outside the box.

One summer day, I rode my black Huffy bicycle up and down Mandy's street. I heard the annoyingly catchy jingle "Turkey in the Straw" echoing from the nearby Good Humor ice cream truck turning the corner. The vintage truck stopped in front of Mandy's house, and kids lined up to get treats. As usual, a group of boys, spanning various ages, had gathered on Mandy's front lawn, with Mandy at the center. I watched and waited until the last kid was served, and the Good Humor driver began to pull away slowly. Seizing the moment, I swiftly dismounted my bike and stealthily hopped onto the truck's back bumper, unnoticed by the driver.

That immediately got the kids' attention—including Mandy. Conversations stopped, and heads turned my way.

As the truck leisurely drove down the block and the driver re-started the mechanical chimes to play the "Turkey in the Straw" song, I opened the back freezer door where the ice cream was kept. I reached in, grabbed a handful of frozen treats, and began slinging the goodies one by one to kids following the van on foot or bike. Boys and girls were scrambling down Mandy's block, trying to catch what I tossed them as Mandy looked on.

My impromptu ice cream distribution caught Mandy's eye, proving that sometimes daring acts pay off. My audacity impressed her, sparking her curiosity and desire to know more about me.

Soon after that incident, we began to see each other as boyfriend and girlfriend. Our dates mainly consisted of Mandy and me hanging out on her front porch, with a dozen other boys showing up vying for her attention. Some kids were older and bigger than me and could easily crush me in a fight, so I wasn't sure how to convince them to scram and leave Mandy and me alone. I needed assistance.

Enter Anthony Romano.

Anthony was a happy-go-lucky man-child my age whom I had known by sight for years but had never spoken to. We played youth football in the league his father created in our hometown. Like every Italian kid I knew at the time, Anthony was fully developed and looked twenty. He had hulking muscles, a mustache way more than peach fuzz, thick beard stubble like poppy seeds on a bagel, hairy arms and legs, and a baritone voice. A good-natured person, he was the best football player in our rec league and was as fast as lightning and strong as a gorilla. Everyone liked and respected Anthony, not out of fear of him but because he was one of the nicest kids in school. When I informed Anthony of my dilemma, he understood the importance of my relationship with Mandy and offered to help. He asked the other boys to respect our privacy, and they did. They willingly dispersed, just like that. Anthony never had to use physical or psychological intimidation, just his niceness. And that began my lifelong friendship with Anthony over the last forty-two years. He was my go-to guy then and has been ever since—my brother from another mother.

The first time Anthony Romano came to call for me at my house, my mother was both confused and concerned. There stood a grown-looking man calling on her youngest son, a boy of only thirteen who looked ten. She asked Anthony to repeat who he was there to see. Was it Brother 1, aged twenty-three? Or was it Brother 2, aged sixteen? Anthony replied that he was calling for *me*.

Believing him to be a child molester, she questioned what he wanted with me. Anthony smiled broadly and claimed he wanted to play with me. My mom took a step backward toward our kitchen wall phone, preparing to call the police before she asked his name and age. Anthony stated his name with a goofy grin on his olive-skinned, poppy-seed, stubbled face and answered, "Thirteen." My mother's jaw dropped. Recognizing his last name, she exhaled and allowed Anthony entrance, remarking that he looked like an adult.

Anthony wasn't the only kid with whom I'd become lifelong friends. In seventh grade, my neighborhood friend Billy Benson, who lived up the block four homes, told me he was friends with a Turkish kid named Mehmet Hikmet, whom I had to meet. My first question was, "What's a Turkish kid?" Billy explained.

Billy wanted me to meet Mehmet because, like me, Mehmet had a few screws loose, and Billy thought we should become friends. It was only natural. It would be like Lennon meeting McCartney. Or peanut butter meeting jelly.

Mehmet lived in another development, an upscale one, a seven-minute bike ride away. Billy had an unusual request in how he wanted me to meet his Turkish friend. He wanted me to jump him. Jumping kids was a popular pastime with some dimwitted boys in my middle school, of which I was one. Without warning, you'd jump on some unsuspecting boy and start slapping and kicking him. It sounded like a great idea to a thirteen-year-old moron, so I said yes.

One day in school, Mehmet was standing at his hallway locker in between periods, working on unlocking his combination padlock, when I pounced. Billy watched the spectacle unfold from across the hall, giggling at the sight. Bewildered as to what was happening, Mehmet fought back as I slapped and kicked him. We tussled, and I realized that while I had speed on him, he was quite a strong Turkish kid. After Mehmet managed to get me off him, Billy showed up sporting a Cheshire grin and introduced us properly to one another, with Mehmet and me both out of breath from the brief tussle. That began my lifelong friendship with Mehmet these last forty-two years. Like Anthony, I consider Mehmet a brother from another mother. The unusual way we met always provides an interesting story whenever people ask how we became friends.

With my newfound friends—my new brothers—my adolescent years were a montage of playing pick-up sports or games in the neighborhood. We adventured in the woods, rode our bikes—or, for those who had them, mopeds—around town, played ball on my basketball court, sledded down sloped hills on our Flexible Flyers after snowfalls, and enjoyed the latest arcade games at The Pantry or the Soda Queen mini-mart. But I also did some unusual things, too.

My oldest brother, Brother 1, kept a long black cassock in his bedroom, which he had worn ten years before when he served mass as an altar boy at St. Mary's church. When I was thirteen, I snooped in his room and snatched it from his closet. I knew I wanted to use it somehow, but I wasn't exactly sure how. Then, it hit me, and I came up with what I thought was a brilliant idea.

I rounded up a dozen neighborhood kids and told them to meet me after school at the main entrance to our development. The road that led to my development had an open meadow with a great green expanse of grass on one side. And beyond that were acres of cornfield. One day after the yellow school bus deposited us back in our development, twelve or so of my schoolmates convened at the designated spot, questioning me about what I had planned.

Before the audience, I slipped into the black cassock and held large wooden replicas of the Ten Commandments tablets—a former art project Brother 1 made years before—

that I also lifted from my brother's closet. I positioned the kids around me in a semi-circle. I instructed them to bow to me, raise their hands, and wave them around as I gave my impromptu performance, occasionally holding the Ten Commandments tablets above my head. As you can imagine, my dashing improvisations created quite a spectacle. Vehicles driving by slowed to a crawl as passengers eyed the scene curiously. People gathered and watched from across the street with stunned amusement. Some folks laughed, some cursed, some told us we were going to hell, and others honked their car horns—lots of confusion. After about fifteen minutes and not wanting to get chased away, we scattered from the scene.

    We met several more days over the next few weeks on different days and times to avoid interrogation until the cops visited us one afternoon. By then, the crowd had grown to more than twenty curious kids, all wanting to be part of the comical gathering. When the police showed up, boys and girls took off in different directions, like cockroaches when a light was turned on. Good luck trying to catch teenagers fleeing on foot. The lone officer who showed up focused his attention on the one nitwit wearing the cassock: me.

    I ran as fast as I could, lifting my ankle-length black robe with both hands, running first through the meadow and then through the cornfield, adrenaline coursing through my body. More than once, I stopped to suck air, bent in half as I did. Luckily, I was never caught and remain at large some forty-plus years later. And the legend of my nuttiness grew.

    I was at a party at a friend's house a few years back. I was talking to my wife and another couple when a woman about my age approached me and asked if I was the kid who 'donned the priest uniform' and conducted those mock religious ceremonies outside my old development decades before. I glanced at my wife, smiled, looked back at the woman, and acknowledged that I was. Her face lit up like a pinball machine. "Oh, shit," she replied, laughing cautiously. "My little brother was in the crowd during some of your performances." She asked what I was doing for a living. I told her I was a priest . . . and that I was joking.

I often tell people I could win a Nobel Peace Prize, a Pulitzer Prize, an Oscar, a Super Bowl MVP, a Grammy, an Emmy, a Tony, cure cancer, end world hunger, and create peace in the Middle East. Yet, people would best remember me as the kooky kid who wore a priest uniform and conducted fake religious ceremonies circa 1977 outside my Geneva development.

In retrospect, I was creating what artists today call *performance art*. I just didn't know it at the time. It was before the term became part of the American lexicon.

CHAPTER 4

You Like . . . *Me*?

The world I had created outside my turbulent home made me proud. I was an odd kid but created a new set of brothers. I entertained them, they enjoyed me, and I appreciated them. We explored the woods, played sports, and often slept over at each other's homes on the weekends. I managed my asthma to excel in youth basketball, baseball, football, and the annual Punt, Pass & Kick competitions, where I received 2nd Place silver trophies multiple years in a row. But my home life wasn't good. My parents fought nearly every night: before my father went to the American Legion and when he arrived home drunk after it closed.

Lonely and longing for sibling companionship, I received none. My brothers and sister were all living their own lives without me. Moreover, I was both heartbroken and resentful that my father wanted nothing to do with me. Or anyone else, for that matter. As I got deeper into my teen years, I learned why he was the way he was. My mom surprisingly opened up and candidly told me his story one day since I had been peppering her with questions about his desire to get drunk each night and the resulting behavior. Though it didn't diminish my fear of him, it did help solve the *why* factor of his actions.

    First off, I learned that my father grew up without a father. That was surprising to hear. His father split after my dad was born, and his uncle and aunt raised him. His mother was very young and too busy with her aspiring political career lobbying her Democrat party's base to vote for Fiorello LaGuardia, New York City's longtime and popular Republican mayor whose name is now synonymous with the airport in Queens. My paternal grandmother reportedly hobnobbed with Mayor LaGuardia and Presidential First Lady Eleanor Roosevelt, among other notable political luminaries of the day with ties to New York politics. My mother showed me several press photos I'd never seen of my grandmother—a woman I had never met, and my father rarely saw himself—standing at podiums next to First Lady Roosevelt and seated next to New York City Mayor La Guardia and his eventual successor, Mayor O'Dwyer. While shunning my father when he was a boy was unconscionable and unmotherly, it was impressive who she aided.

    My dad never experienced firsthand what a father's role should be in raising a son. There was no template for him to copy. And because he rarely saw his mother, he received limited maternal nurturing from her. In addition, my father was naturally quiet, with low energy output and an aversion to being social—unlike his outgoing mother. Due to my father's social limitations and desire to be alone, it may not have been the best idea for him to marry and start a family. He was way over his head, entering into a marriage with a wife and having four kids spread out over thirteen years afterward. As with all kids, each of his children was challenging in some way—emotionally, financially, and otherwise. It must have been overwhelming for the guy. Because my father was not a communicator, he let his frustrations build up inside for years until he developed a seething resentment for his family. To deal with his miserable existence and pain, he chose to drink beer—lots of it. And then he'd explode.

My mother told me that the first time my father ever saw his father was in Puerto Rico when my parents lived there in the 1950s. My father was in his thirties and trying to get his computer business off the ground. Word got back to my dad that his father was living in a little cabin in the Sierra de Luquillo mountains in the northwest part of the island. One day, my father decided to drive an unpaved dirt road up the mountain to pay him an unannounced visit.

Upon arriving at the dilapidated ranch—one of a few stilted shacks clinging to a steep mountainside slope—my dad knocked on the flimsily built door. A minute later, the door creaked open. A spitting image of my father—twenty years older—appeared at the threshold. Their eyes locked on each other, neither man speaking a word. After a few moments, my father turned around and left. I guess he got what he was after. According to my mother, that brief meeting was the first and last time my dad saw his father. When he returned home, my mother said it was the only time she ever saw him cry. I'm not sure if that's entirely accurate. I'm confident my dad checked my high school report cards. They would have made him cry.

Speaking of crying . . . By the time I became a teen, my father had already broken my heart too many times to count. I prayed to God and Jesus every night, asking for their help to get my father to like me first and then love me eventually. But my nightly prayers and requests for help went unanswered. I wept in silence in bed, wondering why my dad didn't like me and why we couldn't have the father-son relationship I so desired and that my friends had with their fathers. I was wounded more than I could ever express. And just when I thought I could not be hurt more, my father managed to destroy me. I was fourteen and in the eighth grade.

When he was young, my father was a skilled basketball player. He played in high school at the well-known Cardinal Hayes in the Bronx. When he was older, despite being an alcoholic during my formative years, my dad managed to coach youth basketball for years. A functioning alcoholic, they call it. I inherited my dad's athletic gene, excelling in football, baseball, and basketball. So, it was no surprise that I was an all-star on the traveling youth basketball team every year, playing with the top kids in our region of New Jersey. Then, one year, my father became the team's head coach.

As was customary at the end of the basketball season, the two best kids from each of the league's dozen teams were selected to try out for the traveling all-star team. The best players would travel to neighboring towns and compete against those towns' all-stars. Twenty-four kids auditioned for the team's eight available spots—five starters and three backups. At that age, I was arguably the fourth or the fifth-best kid out of the two dozen who tried out. Not only should I have easily made the cut to eight, but I should have been one of the team's five starting players.

After a near-flawless audition, I was confident my performance on the court would earn me a spot on the team—not because my dad was the coach. After the tryout, kids approached me and congratulated me for my excellent performance. I thanked them and wished them all good luck. Most of these players were my friends.

My father blew his whistle and instructed all twenty-four players to stand shoulder to shoulder in a single line at the half-court line. Those selected would be called to take a step forward. My father announced the first name. Drew took a single step forward. He was the best player, so it was no surprise he was the first pick. My dad called out the next name, Sage. No surprise there, either. He was the second-best player out of the group. And then he called the next name after that. And then the next name was announced. Standing among the non-chosen, I was silently doing the math, trying to figure out how many picks were left.

And then my father called out the next kid's name. The boy stepped forward. I knew I was much better than him. So did the other players. *What's happening here?* I wondered, panicking.

And then the next kid's name was called. Shocked, the boy looked around before stepping forward. I was considerably better than that kid, too. Players eyeballed each other and me, wondering why I was still among those unselected after six names had been called and only two spots left. Whispers made their way up and down the line. My dad blew his whistle to restore order. He waited momentarily before calling the next boy's name to step forward. He did. Only one spot was left. My heart was pounding. All I could do was stand there and breathe to maintain composure. The only thought running through my head was *He's making me sweat it out because I'm his son.*

And then my father called out the last player's name to step forward, making his final selection to the team. Much to my chagrin, my name was not announced. My mouth hung open among the other unselected sixteen kids, feeling like a mule kicked me in the chest.

Silence befell the group before the kids turned to each other, and chatter began among the players. I was devastated. Misty-eyed, I looked at my father. When our eyes met, he looked away. Even the players who made the team and knew I was better than them awkwardly approached me to apologize, which was kind of them. But it only further deepened my embarrassment. Head down and feeling like a balloon that had just been drained of its air, I quietly shuffled past my peers into the locker room to get changed. The ride home with my father was yet another silent one. I didn't want to give him the satisfaction of seeing me cry, so I did my best to dam up all the tears wanting to burst out. I sat stewing, staring out the window, wishing I was out there. Somewhere, anywhere, it didn't matter. I'll take it. When I got home, I reported the news to my mother before bolting from the house and heading back to my fort in the woods. That was one of my hideaways where I'd escape the world when things got tough.

My mom was fuming and questioned my father on how and why he didn't pick his son, who was one of the five best players in the league, one of its top scorers, top defenders, top assists leaders, and best rebounders. His response: "I didn't want people to think nepotism played a role in me choosing Michael."

My mother reminded him about my accomplishments that season, including winning a league award and being my division's top scorer. As if that weren't enough, she mentioned that I had made the all-star team the last three years in a row — before he became the coach.

None of that mattered. My father's decision was final, and I had to live with it.

My father's actions had a much deeper meaning than me just being cut from some traveling all-star youth basketball team. It was yet another symbolic reminder of him cutting me out of his life.

D

I wasn't interested in girls until I met Mandy in the summer when I was going into eighth grade. If a girl liked me or called for me at my home, I'd send her away, thinking it was strange and wondering why she showed any interest in me. With Mandy, that all changed. My hormones started kicking in, and my thoughts shifted into overdrive. I couldn't stop thinking about girls. Although Mandy and I shared a fantastic summer between seventh and eighth grade, she attended a different school that fall, and we never saw each other again.

While playing on the eighth-grade basketball team, a breathtakingly beautiful cheerleader caught my eye and captured my heart: another eighth-grader whose name I learned was Domonique Bianchi.

If you combined fourteen-year-old versions of Natalie Wood and Adrienne Barbeau, you'd have Domonique: long dark hair, big brown doe eyes, a wide white smile, and a pretty nose. Domonique did not have a single pimple on her face, wore no braces, and had a petite body. The girl was perfect. I was in love. Not puppy love—*love*. Way beyond anything I'd ever felt for Mandy and her incredibly developed body the summer before. And for some odd reason, out of all the handsome and athletic boys on the team, Domonique liked me. Not handsome Drew, whom all the girls swooned over. Not cute, wise-guy Kurt. And not the recently-arrived-from-Southern-California blond-haired, blue-eyed Sage, who looked and was built like a Norse god. She liked awkward, undeveloped, weird, gangly me. I struggled to process that. This was the second attractive girl who liked me in the past year, and I could not figure out why. Domonique was incandescent and lit up a room. She was like a magnetic field; everybody was drawn to her: boys, girls, teachers, parents, coaches—everyone, including me.

As was customary back then, I formally asked Domonique out face-to-face ("Would you go out with me?"). She said yes, and we became inseparable during the rest of our school year. In school, I carried her books and kissed her goodbye at her classroom door before bolting to my own class, flying high on Cloud Nine along the way, my black Converse Chuck Taylor All-Star sneakers not once touching the floor. After school and during basketball practice, we'd talk, hold hands, and sneak kisses during breaks in the gymnasium—she as a cheerleader for the team and me as a player on it. After school, some days, I'd walk Domonique home through the trail in the woods behind our junior high school. We'd hang out at her ranch house and watch TV, kiss, hold hands, cop feels off each other and make each other giggle. It was pure ecstasy. Life rolled merrily with Domonique. She was kind, attentive, funny, sweet, and incredibly easy to get along with. She was an angel who made up for whatever bad things were happening at home and the lack of attention I received there.

    I'd never experienced happiness on that level before. It was overwhelming and difficult to process. Early in my relationship with Domonique, I asked her why she liked me. She said I was cute and funny and that I made her laugh. Domonique knew about my eccentricities, faults, weird appetites, attention deficits, and OCD behaviors, and she still chose me over the other boys. While my mother loved me and my friends enjoyed me, Domonique was the only person who believed in me. That was huge.

    At that time, it was popular for boyfriends and girlfriends to give each other hickeys. They were bruise-like marks caused by sucking the skin on the neck. You'd suck hard enough to burst small superficial blood vessels under the skin, which would then create a silver dollar-sized mark kids would wear as a badge of honor. Yup, Mike got himself a hickey. Domonique must dig him! While dating, I'd only heard of hickeys but had no idea what they were or how they were given or received. One day, while sitting on her Colonial-style wingback couch in her family room watching TV, Domonique whispered to me that she wanted to give me a hickey before her mom returned home from work. Confused and thinking it was something completely different—something I saw in one of my brother's girly magazines—I said OK.

I stood up from her couch in the TV room, glanced around, and began to unzip the zipper on my Levi's jeans.

Domonique gave me a look like *What are you doing*? I shrugged, zipped up my pants, and sat back on her couch. Domonique then began kissing my neck. It was ticklish at first. Then she clamped down with her perfect white teeth and started simultaneously biting and sucking my neck. *Is this a hickey?* I questioned. It felt odd and hurt. Not so much fun. But if Domonique was giving it, I happily obliged to take it. The bruise lasted a few days, and I proudly wore it around the school. At home, I covered it with one of the many turtlenecks or dickeys I wore then.

D

Still struggling to figure out why my brain was not processing information when reading, I acted out with childish buffoonery and shenanigans to mask my unwanted challenges. As a result, I didn't get much playing time on the eighth-grade basketball team. Though my behavior entertained my peers, it irked my coaches. My coaches liked me, but they didn't take me seriously. Throughout the season, I gave them too many reasons not to. The final straw that broke the camel's back was when they put me into a game with only a few minutes left, and I decided to clown around.

I was so skinny that I wore a shoelace tied tight around my thin waist to keep my team shorts from falling off. While positioning myself for a rebound underneath the basket, I loosened the knot on my makeshift belt, waiting for the right moment to give it a final tug. That moment came a few seconds later when an opposing player rebounded the ball.

I yanked the shoelace, my shorts instantly dropped to my ankles, and I stepped out of them. There I stood, my bare white ass and jockstrap hiding my prepubescent genitals. Players on both teams were surprised, their mouths ajar, trying to process what was happening. A collective gasp of astonishment spread across the sparse crowd in the gymnasium, glimpsing the strange sight. While players stood frozen in shock, I snatched the ball from the dumbfounded kid on the opposing team and dribbled down the court bare-assed like nothing was wrong, my cheeks whiter than a fresh snowfall. I felt like Moses parting the Red Sea of bewildered kids darting out of my way. Both benches stood, guffawing and hollering, my coaches glaring at me. The referee blew his whistle between chuckles, trying to halt the action. Undeterred, I kept dribbling toward the basket and scored an uncontested layup. It was the easiest basket of my life. The ref finally caught up to me and called a technical foul, ejecting me from the game. Suppressing their laughter, my coaches barked at me to put my shorts back on and get the hell off the court. With a straight face, I pretended not to know what was happening, shrugging, my hands outstretched with palms facing up while walking off the court.

I'd caused quite a sensation, that was for sure. Once off the court, my head coach ordered me to the locker room. A few seconds later, the metal locker room door busted open. When I peeked around the corner to see who entered, my team shorts hit me in the face. They were thrown by my head coach, Mr. Sampson. A moment later, I received a good talking to by the head coach and his two assistants. I apologized to them and was forced to apologize to each team member, which I did. Was it worth it? At the time, it was.

At the game's end, nobody was talking about how Drew scored eighteen points yet kept the other team's star player he guarded to only four. No one spoke about Sage's fifteen rebounds that helped our team keep possession of the ball. Nobody was talking about Greg Goldstein's ten points and ten assists—called a double-double. And nobody was talking about how our team won by crushing another opponent in our conference. In the days after the infamous game, kids in school and around town talked about my buffoonery. Boys I didn't know were congratulating me and patting me on the back as I walked down the hallways. Girls who'd never noticed me before were throwing flirtatious smiles my way. I would undoubtedly have been a YouTube sensation if they had social media and cell phones back then. My video would have gone viral, racking up millions of views worldwide. I'd have a new moniker: *Bare-assed boy dribbling basketball.* I'd secure an agent and a publicist, appear on talk shows, and land a reality TV show with other teen morons. I'd be invited to speak at NAMBLA conventions in San Francisco. I'd become famous for fifteen minutes and make millions of dollars that I'd quickly blow paying for my large posse of hangers-on, buying albino tigers, renting a private circus in my backyard, purchasing a fleet of go-karts and dirt bikes, and hiring Ettore Boiardi—Chef Boyardee's real name—to personally prepare my meals, instead of having to eat his slop from a can. And like so many other numbskulls, I'd sue my parents, end up in bankruptcy court, and of course, eventually in drug and alcohol rehab.

Here's a list of other antics that undoubtedly put gray hair on my coaches' heads and relegated my backside to a wooden bleacher for the rest of my eighth-grade basketball season.

- While riding on the bus during away games, I'd tie my jockstrap to a fishing line and dangle it out an open bus

window, blowing around for passing cars to see. My teammates would giggle, cars would beep, and my coaches, gnashing their teeth, would bark at me to pull it back inside.
- During practice, when the coaches weren't looking, I'd enlist a teammate to get on his hands and knees near the basket. Then I'd dribble from beyond the foul line, pick up speed, and jump on my teammate's back to vault myself higher to slam dunk.
- During suicide drills one day, I poured hydrosulfate into a fan. Within seconds, the gymnasium smelled like rotten eggs, causing everyone to gag—including me. Practice was halted, and we had to evacuate the gym immediately. The gym stunk for two days and was off-limits to anyone then. I confessed to the incident, yet miraculously, was not suspended. However, I was given detention and placed on probation.

Years later, as an adult, I was invited to speak to classes at my high school for a career day. I bumped into my old eighth-grade basketball coach inside the main office. Mr. Sampson had recently transferred to teaching high school kids and was an assistant coach for the boys' varsity basketball team. Although he had less hair on his head, was longer in the tooth, and a good thirty pounds heavier, he had the same handsome face I remembered. After a few moments of him struggling to process who I was and match my name with a kid he hadn't seen in more than twenty years, his face became lucid. He brought up that bare-ass story and commented that it was one of the funniest things he'd seen in his years of coaching youth sports, although at the time, he wanted to strangle me.

As you can see, I possessed a knack for mischief that many of my immature classmates found hilarious and even admirable. Though I wasn't receiving attention at home, I got it at school and on the basketball team. But in the process, I alienated many of my teammates. And by angering my coaches with disruptive behavior not conducive to the team's greater goal of winning games, I gave up hope for any future playing time—not just in junior high, but in high school. My coaches rightfully punished my behavior by reserving a seat for me beside them on the wooden bleacher to watch games.

    Bench-sitting aside, I did have my best basketball season ever because of Domonique. She cheered the team on as I gazed at her from the bench, admiring her prancing around in that cute little uniform. I could barely take my eyes off her. During away games, Domonique and I were granted the back seat of the bus for privacy, which my teammates always reserved for us. I was honored and thankful for their thoughtfulness. Domonique and I held hands and quickly kissed when no one was watching, savoring those sweet moments, wishing time could stand still. The farther away the opponent, the more time I spent with Domonique on that yellow school bus. They were some of the best days not only of my childhood but also of my life. Domonique got a kick out of my wacky ways and enjoyed my odd sense of humor. I adored her.

I've been moved four times in life: once with Domonique, once when I met my wife, once when I watched my first UFC event on video cassette, and once when I first heard a Beatles album. I was fourteen and in eighth grade when I sat mesmerized and listened to *Meet the Beatles!* I was hooked. After that, I borrowed more albums from my older brother and played them nonstop. Other than Domonique, it was the greatest thing that had happened to me at the time. Like millions of people around the globe, I was enthralled listening to the Fab Four's music. It stirred something deep inside my soul. Not being satisfied as a mere listener—anyone could do that—I needed to teach myself how to *play* their music. George Harrison instantly became my favorite Beatle, so I knew exactly what to do.

    I saved enough money from my previous years of work delivering newspapers, raking leaves, shoveling snow, skimming pools, and singing Christmas carols door-to-door for tips during the holiday season to purchase my first guitar. My mother drove me to Caiazzo's Music on South Street in Freehold, where I bought a used 1964 Gretsch 6186 Clipper hollow-body electric guitar for $200. The music store manager threw in a Mel Bay book on guitar chords, which was nice of him. It wasn't George Harrison's Country Gentleman model Gretsch but a Gretsch nonetheless.

    Here's a fun fact: Bruce Springsteen and I bought our first guitars at Caiazzo's Music in Freehold! Knowing that I bought a guitar from the same small music store as one of the most celebrated stars in rock history is pretty cool for a lifelong Bruce fan like me.

    Soon after I purchased my Gretsch, I bought a small Peavey Backstage 30 amplifier to electrify the music I played. From morning before school, until my eyes shut for bed at night, I taught myself how to play that guitar, practicing numerous hours each day until my fingertips bled. I listened to all the Beatles albums I could get my hands on—from the early records straight through to *Abbey Road* and *Let It Be*—and then taught myself, by ear, how to play the guitar, bass, and other lead parts to their songs. I dissected their music and, note by note, painstakingly learned how to replicate each part. Within six months, I was able to perform most of their tunes. My dilemma was that it was 1978, and The Beatles had broken up eight years before. Punk rock and new wave music were all the rage with my generation then. When trying to impress listeners with my guitar-playing abilities, I performed Beatles music—cool between 1963 and 1970—not so cool in 1978. People were somewhat perplexed after listening to me play a few songs of The Fab Four. They'd stare at my Beatles haircut and Beatles boots on my feet—yes, I often wore them!—and question me if I was auditioning to be a member of some Beatles tribute group. When I told them no, they asked if I could play a popular *current* song by contemporary artists like The Cars, Foreigner, Elvis Costello, The Ramones, The Police, The Clash, or The Talking Heads instead. I gave in and branched out to learn how to play songs from such musical artists, much to the appreciation of my audience.

D

The summer between eighth and ninth grade, a metamorphosis occurred with my body. I broke out with zits all over my face, neck, back, and chest. It was awful. It appeared as if I'd been shot at by a firing squad of marksmen, all shooting red paintballs. If that wasn't enough, I had braces on my upper and lower teeth. I also grew a few inches taller yet failed to gain a single pound. It was a triple-whammy of appearance adjusters that led to deep insecurity. I needed to escape somewhere far away where I could hide. My development's woods were not far enough away. I needed someplace much farther away.

Fortunately, my eighth-grade graduation present was a two-week stay at a basketball camp in the Pocono Mountains in Pennsylvania. It was called the Pocono Invitational Basketball Camp, located in East Stroudsburg. And by *invitational,* they meant whoever could pay the four hundred dollar camp fee was invited. That opportunity could not have come at a better time with my appearance all jacked up. My mom knew my dad's drinking and subsequent behavior were escalating and creating turmoil for me at home, so she decided it would be good for me to be somewhere far away.

I attended camp with four of my closest basketball friends: Kurt Sullivan, Drew Collins, Randy Gibbons, and Jack Buckley. My best friend Michael Michaels was scheduled to join but had to cancel at the last minute due to coming down with chickenpox. Once at camp, my friends and I shared a cabin and participated in drills, scrimmages, games, and other basketball-related activities led by former and current NBA players and coaches. While most kids were homesick and couldn't wait to get back to their families, I questioned camp officials how much it would cost for me to stay there permanently. I never received an answer.

Unfortunately for my fellow campers, I didn't just participate in basketball activities. I still had a mind for mischief, and that mind for mischief nearly got all of us kicked out of basketball camp.

Every small cabin was assigned a number. And each cabin was provided a schedule that pitted cabin versus cabin competing against each other. That schedule was posted on a large board in the main rec room for all to see who, when, and where they were playing. (Example: Cabin 6 vs. Cabin 11 on Court 4 at 11 a.m.) Such information tipped me off as to when particular cabins would be vacant. While Cabins 6 and 11 were playing each other, I'd slip away from my friends and ransack Cabins 6 and 11 rather than watch the game with my cabinmates to learn about future opponents. I'd loot and take my booty back to my cabin and hide the stolen goods: mostly candy, T-shirts, and gym shorts—sought-after items for a thieving teen male. My plundering became rampant, and campers began complaining to camp officials. As a result, camp management made daily P.A. announcements over the loudspeakers, declaring that security would search each of the twenty-five cabins if all the stolen items were not immediately returned. These announcements occurred a few times a day. Whoever was in possession of stolen items would be booted from camp and arrested by the police. They were serious. I nearly shat my pants each time I heard those announcements.

I had told only Drew about my shenanigans, as he was my closest friend at camp. But in no time, every cabin member knew of my actions. My buddies were incredibly upset, claiming they didn't want to be ejected from basketball camp due to my selfish and criminal behavior. My cabin mates were there to become better basketball players and play in high school and perhaps college. I was there to escape my father, hide my pimpled face, my mouth full of silver braces, and my tall stick figure from the eyes of others back home—including Domonique.

My friends were right. I was being a selfish asshole. I apologized and promised to stop if they helped me hide the stolen items before our cabin was randomly searched. Fortunately, they agreed.

While my friends provided lookout, I gathered the stolen items, minus the candy, which had been devoured. There were a dozen T-shirts and a half dozen gym shorts, eighteen items in total. I stashed three items in each of the six pillows on our beds. I realized the pillow itself had a zipper that opened when I removed a pillowcase from a pillow. I carefully stuffed the neatly folded clothing inside each pillow before fluffing it up to make it look natural, zipping it shut, and gently placing the pillow inside each pillowcase.

When we heard the knock on our door, my cabin mates looked at me, shaking their heads.

I gulped.

We were all anxiety-ridden but had to act cool so as not to appear guilty.

Three incredibly tall adult security members—camp counselors in their early twenties—entered our cabin sporting no-nonsense looks. While I stood masking my fear, the counselors painstakingly searched the drawers, closets, duffel bags, rafters, underneath the cabin, a crawl space, and under beds and mattresses. They looked everywhere! Everywhere except *inside* the pillows themselves. After ten minutes, they left our cabin and proceeded to the next one. Crisis and soiled underpants averted, we collectively exhaled.

When I returned home, the legend of my mischievousness grew. Instead of people talking about how well Drew played during camp, how cool it was that Kurt got to shoot baskets one-on-one with an NBA all-star, and how much better Jack became at free-throw shooting, kids were talking about what crazy antics I did during those two weeks.

CHAPTER 5

Name That Tune

Being Catholic was vital to my mother. She was raised in a strict Catholic environment, not only by her parents but by the nuns and priests who beat it . . . uh, I mean, taught her in school. As mentioned, she was a Catholic school product from first grade through graduating from Good Counsel College in White Plains, New York. So, it mattered for my mother to have her children follow in her Catholic footsteps.

My sister attended Catholic high school, Brother 1 attended Catholic high school, and Brother 2 attended Catholic high school for three years before switching to the public high school in our hometown of Geneva. The table had been set for me.

After leaving St. Mary's Elementary School and graduating from public middle school, it was time for me to choose a high school. At my mother's urging, I applied to St.

John Vianney in Holmdel, a few towns away. However, I was not accepted because I didn't pass the entrance exam. It was a timed test, and I struggled to take timed tests due to my reading comprehension issues. In addition, I had great difficulty retaining what I'd read after reading it. Those two deficits lessened my chances of passing any timed test.

When my mother found out I was not accepted, she was upset. Not at me for failing the test but at St. John's for not accepting me. How dare they not accept her Catholic son!

Rejection letter in her bejeweled hand, she drove to the high school and demanded to meet with Father John, the school's cantankerous principal. Somehow, she was granted the unplanned meeting and made an impassioned plea to the priest, enlightening him on just how good a Catholic family we were—she never missed a Sunday mass, she and her husband graduated from Catholic high schools and colleges, all her other children attended Catholic high schools, blah blah blah. After my mother made her convincing case, Father John surprisingly reversed his decision. I was accepted into St. John's. Victory for mom. The only problem was that I had changed my mind while my mother was busy pleading her case to Father John. I didn't want to go to St. John Vianney High School. What can I say? I was a fourteen-year-old moron. My girlfriend, Domonique, would be attending my hometown high school, as would all my friends. I didn't want another St. Mary's situation like the one I experienced when I went outside my hometown, where I had little in common with my classmates from other towns. Plus, I was madly in love with Domonique and couldn't abandon her. I had to break the news to my mom that I did not want to go to St. John's. I was determined to go to the public Geneva High School.

After I made my feelings known, my mom was shocked. And angry. She was just as upset at me as when I fell asleep at the circus as a child. But she was also disappointed, which ripped my heart in two. Despite my mother's feelings, she supported my decision. The bewildering thing was—are you ready?—one week into my freshman year in public high school, I broke up with Domonique.

You read that right.

A preemptive move, you could say.

Mind you, I was still head over heels in love with Domonique. However, I had significant insecurities about my appearance then and felt utterly undeserving of her company. In my poorly-wired teenage brain, those insecurities trumped my love for Domonique.

After my sudden appearance changes due to puberty, I wholeheartedly believed that Dominique would break up with me at any minute. And why wouldn't she? I had a face reminiscent of a greasy pepperoni pizza, a mouth filled with silver braces, and a tall body resembling a spear. My legs were so skinny that to compensate for just how thin they were, I used to wear bulky long underwear—called long johns—over my regular underwear, a thick pair of gray sweatpants on top of my long johns, and then a thick pair of gym shorts over them. And then I'd put my jeans on over all that. It didn't matter if it was a hundred degrees out; that was my dress code every day as a freshman. While the abundance of clothing restricted my ability to move—it often appeared as if I were goose-stepping when I walked—it made my legs look thicker, which was all that mattered to me. But my unusual clothing choice back-fired one day when I got into a fistfight with a kid in my English class named Marc.

He thought I made an offensive remark about him in class. The crude comment was made, but by another kid—not me. Marc approached me after the period and challenged me to a fight because of what he thought I'd said. Though I denied saying it and pointed to the kid who actually did say it, Marc was focused on me. Nothing was going to change his mind, so we decided to scrap. Due to the amount of layers of clothing underneath my jeans, my legs were restricted. It felt like I had leg braces on. Once outside, Marc easily toppled me to the ground and pummeled me while I was rendered immobile. After about two minutes, the school's security guard broke up the scuffle. I got to my feet and dusted myself off, catching my breath before heading to my next class. Regarding the kid I just fought, we became friends for the remainder of high school. And for the boy who framed me, I got back at him by placing a pile of dog shit on his desk seat a few months later. After that, we became friends for the remainder of high school.

As you see, the clothing issue was an everyday obstacle for me. It was a challenge not to be noticed by my classmates when undressing/dressing for gym class in the locker room. I knew if I were ever seen wearing that amount of clothes underneath my jeans, it would be a death sentence to my social status. Instead of being thought of by my classmates as the wacky and mischievous athlete/musician, I'd be considered the laughingstock of the school. So, I became a master of illusion and disappearance by never getting caught changing clothes for gym class. I quickly changed in broom closets, storage rooms, the nurse's office bathroom—anywhere out of view from others.

I told you I was a mess.

Emotionally, I was even worse. I had zero confidence, no self-esteem, and was about as mature as a ten-year-old boy.

Yet Domonique was the opposite. She was beautiful, sweet, mature, and untouched by any signs of puberty. She had not even a single pimple on her beautiful teenage Adrienne Barbeau/Natalie Wood face. The girl was way out of my league. I convinced myself that in no time, all the good-looking upper-class boys would be asking her out, perhaps even my brother. It made sense. Brother 2 was then a senior at my high school after transferring from St. John's and was the varsity football team's starting quarterback and co-captain. He and countless others could offer Domonique much more than I ever could—better looks, a developed body, a car, money, maturity, and confidence. So, I enlisted my close female friend, Stacey Kaplan, to call Domonique and break up with her on my behalf. It made perfect sense to me as an unsophisticated coward.

Stacey phoned Domonique to break the news. At first, Domonique thought it was a joke but quickly realized it was not. After speaking with Stacey, Domonique phoned my home numerous times to gain clarity. My mother answered every time and begged me to talk to the poor girl on the other end of the line. Standing in our orange-painted kitchen with my arms crossed, I refused. Domonique kept questioning my mother why I wouldn't answer her calls. Though I didn't believe it could be possible, I let down my mother even more.

I was an immature chickenshit who didn't know the first thing about how to communicate with someone I adored. My crazy teenage brain kept telling me I should do that.

Of course, the next day in school and the days after that were unbelievably awkward for Domonique and me. I did my best to hide from Domonique and her wide circle of loyal friends, walking the hallways with my head down. And when I did notice her, I averted my eyes and slink away. I could not believe the depths to which I had sunk. I was ashamed of myself. What a rat I was. A cowardly rat.

The day after I had Stacey call Domonique to do my dirty work, I lamented my decision to break up with Domonique. Of course.

A few days later, another freshman named Brandon swooped in and began dating her. And that's when I desperately wanted Domonique back for the rest of freshman year, high school, college, and beyond. I didn't stop loving Domonique, but she never stopped dating Brandon. They dated through the rest of freshman year, high school, and college and stayed together post-college through marriage, kids, and now grandkids. Amazingly, more than forty years later, they're still together. You're welcome, Brandon!

I had two girls baffled and upset by my puzzling actions: my mother when I refused to go to St. John's—after she persuaded the school to reverse their decision and admit me—and Domonique for breaking up with her and by using a surrogate to do my dirty work. To help me get through those messes I created and the pain I caused myself and others, I focused on doing something productive. And that something was music.

Midway through my freshman year, just after finishing playing football on the high school team, I quit the basketball team to form a band. My new best friend Anthony was also teaching himself how to play the guitar, and he was becoming good. We were moving along on the same track. Conveniently, Anthony lived around the block, and we took turns practicing in our respective garages, occasionally performing for curious onlookers who stopped by to see what all the new noise was about. After lots of rehearsing and a dozen cover songs on our set list, we became tighter. But we knew we needed a drummer to have a real rock band. Through our school's grapevine, we heard of a drummer named Tommy, who lived in a nearby development and asked him to join our band. Tommy was a decent drummer and had a look all the girls liked. The only thing I disliked about him was that he carried a comb in his jeans' back pocket. It was large and had a handle, and he constantly whipped it out to run it through his 1970s feathered-styled hair parted in the middle. I knew it was petty of me, but it bothered me. Big time. What guy combed his hair every two minutes? Our new drummer, Tommy, is who. Minus a bass player, we had our band. After mulling over possible names for the band—British

Teeth, The Mongoloids, The Zygotes, The Dung Beatles, and The More Ons (my favorite!)—thanks to Anthony's mother's suggestion, we settled on something less controversial with The Boys.

Like most bands, we started out pretty bad. But with practice, we improved. In time, we performed at a few local gatherings and were eventually hired to play at some girl's eighth-grade graduation party before two dozen strangers, including a handful of girls our age. Performing in front of an audience was an adrenaline rush. In addition, girls our age were in that audience, and getting paid for playing was the deal sealer. That was it. I'd found my life's calling, my eventual career. I was going to become a rock star.

Founding The Boys with Anthony worked wonders for me. It provided me with a sense of purpose, boosted my confidence, and supplied me with the attention I desperately sought yet did not receive from my family members at home. And it got me noticed by some girls in my neighborhood. I still looked a mess: pencil-thin and gangly, all arms and legs, Beatles haircut, zits the size of sewing thimbles on my oily face, braces on my teeth, and bushy eyebrows like giant furry gypsy moths. Yet despite my horrifying appearance, because I was a decently skilled guitarist and was in a rock band, I became attractive to some girls. (Thank you, guitar!) For the remainder of my freshman year, I practiced playing my Gretsch guitar morning, noon, and night. And I became better, learning to play lead solos rather than just rhythm guitar. I immersed myself in music, reading books about rock and roll and blues history, guitar legends, biographies about musicians, and anything about The Beatles, Bruce Springsteen, and Neil Young. And I improved upon the bass, keyboards, and harmonica. I even bought a soprano recorder and taught myself to play parts of certain songs featuring that wind instrument. Rather than do my homework each night, I spent my evening hours practicing music and calling random unwitting students I barely knew to play Name That Tune with them—though none knew they'd be participants in my little game when they got on the phone. I'd look up kids in the phone book; some in my grade, some not. Once I obtained their phone number, I'd call their house. The following is what usually occurred during my Name That Tune calls:

MOTHER'S VOICE: "Hello?"
ME: "Hi, may I speak with Rachel, please?"
MOTHER'S VOICE: "Yes. One moment."
RACHEL, CONFUSED: "Hello?"
ME: "Rachel? Name-this-tune . . ." I'd play between ten to twenty seconds of a popular song of the day and then stop. "Can you name that tune?
RACHEL, MORE CONFUSED: "Who is this?"
ME: "Name that tune, and I'll tell you . . ."

I called boys and girls alike, from freshmen to seniors and from jocks to burnouts to brainiacs; it didn't matter. They were all fair game. Half the kids I called were more interested in knowing *who* was calling them rather than naming the song. The other half tried to name the tune before asking who was calling. For those kids, I told them my name. Sometimes, a conversation would start, and they would compliment my guitar-playing before questioning what the hell I was doing, phoning them. Other times, I'd congratulate them on guessing correctly and hang up. Many couldn't get past who was calling them and were fixated on finding out without trying to name the tune. I'd hang up in those situations and move on to the next person. That was before caller ID and pressing star-something to instantly identify who was calling you, so I remained anonymous.

Some kids got a kick out of my random calls and thought I was nuts, which, of course, I was. *Who does this?* Others were irked, which was understandable. If a concerned parent asked me who was calling before they handed the phone to their son or daughter, I'd often respond, "Goat Dung." They'd always respond with a "Excuse me?" I'd then say, "Bill Dunn," and they'd sigh in relief and say, "Oh, OK. I thought you said something else. Hold on." Other times, I'd make up interesting names like Roger Bergdorf, Sammy Rabinowitz, or Christian L'Enfant, which would further pique the curiosity of the intended recipient once they got on the phone since there were no such named persons in our town. One thing was sure: some school kids were talking about the Name That Tune calls they received the night before and the wacky boy who made them. But it was harmless fun—better than me egging their homes, smashing their homegrown pumpkins, and stealing their belongings. At the expense of my grades, I made countless Name That Tune calls to random kids in my first two years of high school.

As it was for most boys, being fourteen was a rough age for me. My father's drinking was out of control. As a result, it was hard for my mother to keep her eyes focused on me when she was distracted by my father's situation. Plus, at age fourteen, I was a typical boy wanting my privacy to enjoy my older brothers' *Swedish Erotica* magazines. That was hardcore stuff—especially for a kid who had barely made out with a girl. Both my older brothers enjoyed reading porn magazines. Remember, one brother was ten years older than me, the other three years older. In sexual terms, those guys were light years ahead of me. But I learned quickly about sex from those raunchy magazines I lifted from underneath my brothers' mattresses or hidden underneath clothes inside their dresser drawers. When my friends would excitedly show me a *Playboy* or *Penthouse* magazine with one woman's naked breasts exposed, I'd smirk and pull out a copy of *Swedish Erotica* with graphic images and sexual encounters they'd never seen before. My friends would drop their magazines on the floor and stare at what I'd shown them, their mouths ajar and eyes wide as Frisbees. I never got the birds and bees talk from my dad; I got it from *Swedish Erotica*. It was like going from riding a child's vintage pedal car to riding a Ferrari. Just as uncomfortable as I felt being around my mom when I was fourteen, I'm sure she felt just as uncomfortable being around me. Though she never mentioned it, I'm sure she knew why I was in the bathroom six times a day. She'd raised two other sons, so she knew the drill. Don't ask, don't tell. That was our policy long before it became the military's.

During that awkward and hormonal time in my life, my mom and I began to drift apart. I was becoming a man, and she was steadily losing her husband to alcohol. We were heading in separate directions. Although we still loved one another, I never again felt as close to my mother as I did the first thirteen years of my life.

Though I'd been a top athlete in my age group up through the eighth grade, by freshman year, other kids caught up to me, some surpassing me in talent and ability. Some boys had developed more quickly, grew taller, and put on weight when I had not. As a freshman, I was five feet seven and weighed 110 pounds. I was a late bloomer with all things physical and emotional. When I eventually graduated high school, I was five feet eleven and weighed 137 pounds. And two years after that—at age twenty—I'd grow another three inches to become six-feet-two and fill out to be 160 pounds: no weight training, no supplements, no steroids, no changes to my diet. I still ate grilled cheese sandwiches, plain yellow American cheese sandwiches, brownies, Lindens chocolate chip cookies, and drank Carnation Instant Breakfasts and chocolate milk. No fruits, no vegetables, no salad, no seafood, and rarely meat. As a high school freshman, I shifted my focus from sports to music and mischief. I spent more time with Mehmet and Anthony, creating trouble around our neighborhoods while longing for Domonique every day. Since Michael Michaels attended St. John's and gained a new set of friends, we rarely saw each other. We had a great time hanging out or playing basketball on my court when we did.

A few months after I'd broken up with Domonique—with Stacey doing it on my lily-livered behalf—I cried myself to sleep most nights wanting her back. When I slept, I dreamed we were back together. When I'd see Domonique in school walking down the hallways holding hands with her new boyfriend, I was given a heavy dose of sobering reality, and it physically hurt me to witness it.

I loved Domonique.

I wrote songs about Domonique that I played every day on my guitar. I longed for her to come back into my life, and I prayed to God and the universe every day that my wishes would come true. And then, one day, it happened—a Christmas miracle.

CHAPTER 6

American Legion vs. Family

The day after Christmas 1978, I was playing my guitar in my bedroom, performing the latest song I'd written about Domonique. My mother knocked on my bedroom door, gave me a few seconds—the understood code between us at the time—and then poked her head inside the eight-by-eight room. She told me there was a girl on the front porch who wanted to see me.

I sprang to attention and placed my guitar on the bed. *What?*

Sitting bolt upright, I asked my mother who it was. She said she wasn't sure. I questioned what the girl looked like. My mother remarked that she was very pretty, with long black hair and beautiful eyes; she thought it was Domonique.

I took a moment to process what was happening. Could it be true? Was Domonique coming to let me know she missed me just as much as I missed her and wanted me back? I suddenly became lost in a daydream of impending happiness.

Visions of Domonique and I embracing began dancing in my head. It was a Christmas miracle. Thank you, God! Thank you, Jesus! Thank you!

I launched myself from the bed, glanced in the mirror atop my dresser, grimaced at what I saw staring back at me, and quickly ran my hands through my matted-down Beatles haircut circa 1965. I promptly splashed Old Spice cologne on my neck and bolted to the front door, my mother shouting for me to calm down. When I bounded out of the house, filled with excitement, anticipation, and practically out of breath, my friend Mehmet stood alone on my front porch. Confused, I scanned either side of him for Domonique. She was not there. I asked Mehmet who he came with. Mehmet shrugged and said just himself. Believing he was playing a joke, I peeked in the bushes on both sides of the porch steps.

Domonique was nowhere to be found. I stood frozen for a few moments, processing the situation. Then it registered.

Mehmet had long dark hair, like Domonique. All the moms claimed Mehmet had pretty eyes and Dominique had pretty eyes. Mehmet had wide hips, as his body had not yet filled out, and his voice had not yet deepened. And my mother had never met him. It all made sense.

Glad to see my buddy yet monumentally disappointed he was not my ex-girlfriend, I invited Mehmet inside and introduced him to my mother—as a *boy*. My mother greeted him and remarked on how pretty he looked. Uncomfortable at the compliment, Mehmet scrunched his face and followed me back to my bedroom as I was muttering invectives to myself.

It was no Christmas miracle at all—just my Turkish friend Mehmet at my front door.

Dammit!

Because I was an immature kid with a prefrontal cortex that had not fully developed, it often led to poor decision-making and impulsive acts. Like many teen males, I didn't comprehend that the mischievous things I did around my neighborhood had consequences for others. And because I had a disengaged dad and aloof older brothers who treated me as if I were invisible, I had no one to let me know my behavior was unacceptable, help me understand why, teach me how to correct it, and suggest alternatives to it to make sure I got on—and stayed on—a straight and narrow path. I'd commit mischievous acts without owning my actions and would be remorseless afterward. Sure, my mischief grabbed the attention and the laughs of my friends and gained me respect, which, I had to admit, felt empowering. I was known as the crazy kid who did this or that, and people around my town and school were sharing stories of my escapades. I was being talked about.

I was visible.

I'm sure my reputation as a lunatic prevented me from getting bullied. Nobody messed with me, though I was an easy target. I was thin, and my face still resembled Picasso's *Weeping Woman* painting. (Google it, I'll wait . . .)

Some of my worst teen antics included being a peeping Tom. I observed some interesting things and could never look at certain neighbors or their daughters the same way again. I snow-balled or egged homes, cars, and people as they walked their dogs at night. I snuck out my bedroom window and went skinny-dipping in other people's pools after dark, sometimes leaving behind brown floating presents. Like Spiderman, I scaled neighbors' homes, sat on their roofs, and shot bottle rockets from glass Coca-Cola bottles into the street.

When spotted by passersby, I scrambled off the roof to safety. I spray-painted the side of a business or a distant neighbor's home, and that sort of misconduct.

Of course, if someone egged or spray-painted *my* house, or peeped on *my* mom as she took a shower, or left behind brown floating presents in *my* pool, I'd go ballistic. Therein lies the hypocrisy of teenage boys with a penchant for mischief and disconnected wires in their brains. At that pivotal time of my life, I desperately needed guidance from the three older males who occupied the same home as me. But I received none.

Ninth grade saw me struggle academically, physically, and athletically—everywhere except in my ability to play the guitar and conduct mischief. I could not understand why my brain was still not processing information correctly; I could not understand what I'd just read when I read something. I'd have to read a sentence repeatedly, take copious notes, and then move to the following sentence, paragraph, or page. Doing something others appeared to accomplish quite easily was time-consuming and challenging. I could also not fathom why my brain did not allow me to concentrate on the task, no matter the assignment. I would go to my bedroom with every intention of doing homework. I'd stretch, close the bedroom door, turn off the radio, sit at my desk, open my textbook and notebook, have my pen ready, and try my best to start and complete my assignment. Within a few seconds, I'd zone out and sit blankly, looking out the window. And then some noise or image would grab my full attention: a squirrel scampering up a tree—*look, there's a squirrel!*; a red-breasted robin chirping in its nest; a woodpecker relentlessly pecking away at a tree;

the wind making a loose shutter bang against the house; a school bus applying its brakes to stop; the clanging of pots and pans being washed in the kitchen; a car horn beeping out on the street; a leaf blower or lawn mower humming; an airplane flying overhead; a Harley-Davidson rumbling by; kids out on the street playing; or a fly desperately trying to get out a window—and then once outside, desperately trying to get back inside. It could be any movement or sound. I'd get up and investigate what I saw or heard. In the process, I'd leave behind whatever I was supposed to do. I'd rarely find my way back to the initial task. My attention was elsewhere.

When I'd finally wrangle myself in to start the original assignment, usually at the behest of my mother reminding me, I'd repeat the process. I intended to start and complete something, yet I could not because of my attention deficit.

In 1978, ADD had not yet been added to the DSM manual, so it was not yet a known classification outside a small group of child behavior experts. Adults at the time didn't want to hear that a kid couldn't focus. They'd tell you to stop goofing off and pay better attention. In their mind, the problem would be solved.

And in the rare event I found the initiative to start a task, if it involved reading—which was 99 percent of the time—I'd have tremendous difficulty absorbing the words I read. It was a double-whammy.

As a freshman, I played quarterback on the high school football team and struggled to absorb the offensive playbook. Unlike when I played QB in the youth league from age eight until fourteen, where I only needed to memorize a dozen plays and could rely on my athleticism to achieve results, I needed to memorize dozens of complicated plays as a high schooler. The plays were no longer simple; they were pretty sophisticated.

Double-wing Right Quarterback Draw Option.

YZ Slant Right 32 Slot Back Left.
Power Line Right Split Zone Trap.
Slant Cross Double X Motion Wide Right.
36 Double Cross 14 Power Slot Back Left Slip.

For a defective teen brain that struggled to process and retain *Tom Smith has two dogs, one named Candy and one named Cindy*, it was too daunting to grasp forty or fifty highly confusing plays like the ones above. The quarterback is the team's leader, and if he can't grasp the plays, he can't lead his team. He sits on the bench. It's that simple. I'm not saying I was a future Tom Brady or Joe Montana. But my arm strength, quick release, advanced field and peripheral vision, fast legs, and accuracy were superior to the other quarterback vying for the starting job. However, the other kid's maturity and ability to grasp the playbook and execute the complicated plays made him a starter and me his backup. The coaches thought I wasn't studying the playbook at night. Remember: I'd built a reputation as a cut-up kid. When you act like a clown, people treat you like one. They don't take you seriously—even when you are serious. So, my coaches doubted my efforts. But I was studying the playbook. I just couldn't process it. It'd be like giving someone who doesn't speak Chinese a book in Mandarin and asking him to memorize it, quizzing him the next day to see if he had. That guy wouldn't even know what he was reading, let alone be able to retain it and recite it.

As a result of my inability to absorb the offense's playbook—a crucial component of the team's quarterback/lead offensive player—I did not try out for the team during my sophomore year. I quit. My friends, family, and coaches were all surprised. Playing football was my favorite sport. It appealed to me in an almost mythic way. It was about showcasing my talent on a team of brothers and being part of something productive. One cohesive unit working together for a common goal: to win.

On the offensive side of the game, I loved moving the ball down the field and throwing for and running for touchdowns. I enjoyed reading coverage and interpreting defensive schemes, anticipating plays, tossing passes, and knifing through potential tacklers with the possibility of gaining yardage and scoring a touchdown. The thrill of playing football surpassed any mischief I had ever engaged in. It was the most exhilarating thing I'd ever experienced. But after enjoying football for seven years, I'd have no more of the sport. It was my second most significant loss at the time, after Domonique.

Despite my academic deficits, I found one creative way to improve at least one of my failing grades, that being freshman biology.

A classmate named Jerome was a tiny kid, four-ten and 85 pounds. His small size proved to be an advantage to himself, Mehmet, and me—three dummies failing the same biology class. I hatched a plan that incorporated Jerome and Mehmet.

Biology was divided into two sessions rather than a traditional uninterrupted 45-minute period. They called it a split period. The first half was twenty-five minutes. Then we broke for a half-hour lunch before we'd resume for the final twenty minutes. Our fifty-something teacher unwisely kept her student grade book unlocked in her top desk drawer, which was fantastic news.

I scanned the classroom when the bell rang, signaling the end of the first session. Students began filing out the door. The coast was clear when all the students had exited the classroom.

While Mehmet used himself as a decoy to distract the teacher with bogus questions, I helped Jerome shimmy into a small cabinet underneath a sink in the middle of the lab. He fit inside perfectly. I closed the cabinet door and filed out of the room with Mehmet in tow. Jerome waited until he heard our teacher depart the classroom and close and lock the door behind her. As directed, Jerome climbed out of the cabinet, unlocked the door to the classroom, and then slipped out into the crowd of kids in the hallway. With Jerome and Mehmet standing at separate lookout posts in the bustling hallway, I nonchalantly returned to the room, found the grade book, identified the current semester, and, using a blue ink pen, changed all Mehmet's Es to Bs, Jerome's Es to Bs, and my Es to Bs. I placed the grade book back into the drawer precisely as I'd found it and left the room unnoticed. Operation Grade Change went smoothly.

When my report card was mailed home a few weeks later, my mother was stunned. While she wasn't happy with the rest of my grades, she was over the moon that I achieved a B in biology class during the second semester, considering the semester before when I'd received a D.

As with all my freshman classes (except Phys Ed), I achieved poor grades. One class I was failing was Spanish. That was interesting, considering my father spoke Spanish fluently and used it when he lived in Puerto Rico during two separate stints.

At a parent-teacher conference, my mother met with my Spanish teacher, Mrs. Vogel. Mrs. Vogel was ten years older than me and knew Brother 1 well, so she knew my dad was fluent in Spanish. When Mrs. Vogel questioned my mother about how I could be failing Spanish when my father spoke the language fluently, my mother responded, "My husband doesn't speak any Spanish to Michael." She let the thought set in for a moment before finishing up with, "In fact, he doesn't speak much English to Michael, either."

My Spanish teacher later told me she stared at my mother dumbfounded, not knowing how to respond.

Changing the subject, my Spanish teacher informed my mother that I may have Tourette's syndrome since I often made a commotion in class by blurting out names of Turkish people related to Mehmet. Our class could be in the middle of a lesson or a test when the quiet room would suddenly be interrupted by loud barks of "Dervish!" or "Pembah!" or "Fatima!" or "Mustafa!"

My mother was mystified upon hearing that news. She knew I had a screw loose and was different from her three other children, but she'd never heard such blurtations at home. When my mother questioned me about the matter, I grinned mischievously and murmured I didn't know what my Spanish teacher was talking about. I'm pretty sure I threw in a "*Rashid!*" for good measure.

I loved Turkish names. (Still do.) They were so different from anything I'd ever heard before. I ashamedly admit I had a strange attachment to them. Growing up, I was used to hearing the same old recycled names: Tommy, Billy, Bobby, Michael, John, Susan, Amy, Jill, Lisa, Mary, and the sort. Playing youth football one year, there were six Michaels alone on a team of eleven kids. Suddenly, I met this Turkish kid and was introduced to sophisticated names such as Alptekin, Hasan, Osman, Nesrin, Dervish, Sevil, and others. It was like I found gold. And when you find gold, you tell people about it. So I did.

Of course, Mehmet was not so pleased with my fascination with Turkish names. He wanted to keep them under wraps for fear he'd receive unwanted attention being Muslim in a town populated mostly by Christians and Jews.

But I couldn't resist the urge to blurt out those unusual names, much to Mehmet's dismay.

Fast forward a dozen or so years.

When I began dating my wife, I'd often blurt out the name of one of Mehmet's family members during our time together. Confused, my then-girlfriend would look around and ask me if that person had just entered the location we were at. I shook my head and let her in on my quirky fixation. It took her a while, but eventually, she understood my need to say those names.

It's been over forty-two years since I first heard those Turkish names. And I still repeat some of them nearly every day. Much to my wife's delight, I don't shout them anymore.

Since my childhood friend Michael Michaels attended St. John Vianney High School a few towns away, I rarely saw him. As a result, in my freshman year, I bonded with three other kids in my development—my new best friends, Anthony Romano, Bobby Gervasi, and Patrick Walsh. I'd been friends with Anthony since my days dating Mandy. He was a lovable kid, a great athlete, and co-founder of our cover band, The Boys.

Bobby was a chubby and kind soul who lived across the street from Anthony, and Patrick was a cerebral kid with a square noggin who got straight As and lived two blocks away. He was the brightest among us, and I knew he would make something of himself one day. I sometimes wondered why Patrick hung out with us, the hooligans that we were. He often provided the voice of reason and rationale I needed, as if older brothering me.

If I picked up a rock and announced I wanted to throw it at someone's car or house, Patrick would ask me why. Then, calmly and reasonably, he would walk me through the steps to show me all of the damage I would cause the victim and question how I'd feel if someone hurled a rock at *my* home or *my* parents' car. Nine times out of ten, I'd drop the rock. Despite my teenage brain being impervious to logic, Patrick's sensible words somehow managed to seep through.

Between our freshman and sophomore years in high school, Anthony, Bobby, Patrick, and I became a tight-knit unit and spent a fantastic summer together. The Boys' band practiced daily, performed out in public at times, and our foursome played golf. Sharing clubs owned by Anthony and Patrick, we'd catch a ride from anyone with a motor vehicle, then sneak onto the 18-hole golf course in our hometown. We'd hide in the trees behind the fourth-hole tee and wait for the right moment when no one was around. We'd emerge when the coast was clear, quickly tee up our golf balls, and begin our round. Incredibly, we never got caught that summer. We were not even questioned. Not once! Playing golf and spending time with my buddies during our summer break provided me much-needed relief since Domonique was still dating someone else while I still loved her, and my dad's drinking was at an all-time high.

As noted, my dad mentally checked out of our family when I was in the eighth grade. Because he was not a communicator, he never told us why. Perhaps his life didn't turn out how he'd imagined—married with four kids with a home that required grass to be mowed, gutters to be cleaned, and neighbors with whom to socialize. Perhaps it was his job as a computer programmer in Manhattan and the drudgery of his daily commute to and from the unsafe city. Or maybe it was a combination of both or something completely different. Whatever it was, he did not want to be around his family. He made that abundantly clear. While other kids had their dads engaged in their lives, my dad was just about as disengaged as a father who came home every night could be. Rather than family engagement, he chose the American Legion as his refuge away from home.

The American Legion branch in Geneva was an old, dimly lit building with a gravel parking lot four miles from our home. The inside was dark and dingy and exuded sadness and despair. It looked like it hadn't been remodeled since the Truman administration. Aside from smelling like cigarette smoke, there was always a pungent odor of sewage wafting from the single filthy bathroom inside the place, yet no one ever seemed to care to fix it.

The same dozen men—including my father—sat at the same bar every night, served by the same red bulbous-nosed bartender, while a gauzy haze of cigarette smoke floated above them. All the male patrons appeared defeated by their wives and children and the jobs their lives had produced. So they drank their troubles away, giving them more problems than they already had.

During my high school years, my father always drove himself home after long nights imbibing at the American Legion. Sometimes, the family car would be parked crooked on the driveway; sometimes, it was parked on our side lawn, and a few times, it was parked in front of someone else's home down the block. It was a constant source of embarrassment for me. Once, it was parked in our front yard, with all four tires missing—just four rims dug into the fresh zoysia grass we had planted the week before. How all four tires came off and where they ended up remains a mystery. My buddy Mehmet came to call for me one Saturday morning, knocking on my front door. When I greeted him, his eyes were the size of dinner plates. He was chuckling and lost for words, pointing to my family's car parked right smack in the middle of our front yard without any tires. Zero.

I knew how it got there. And why, though I didn't tell Mehmet. This was my dirty family secret.

Hearing a visitor had entered our home, my mother descended the thirteen steps from her upstairs bedroom and greeted Mehmet in our living room, commenting on his pretty eyes. Erasing the smile from his face and deflecting from the compliment, Mehmet pointed to the car parked on our lawn. My mother clenched her jaw, shook her head, and stormed back up the thirteen steps to the spare bedroom where my father was still sleeping and had slept most nights. They exchanged words. A few minutes later, accompanied by my mother, my disheveled dad groggily staggered down the steps in his light blue boxers and white V-neck undershirt, a scowl on his face and still reeking of beer and cigarettes.

He looked outside at the car with four missing tires, shook his head, and denied involvement. Since I was in his sightline, he pointed to me with his long index finger, claiming I did it. My mother reminded him I was only fifteen and didn't drive, my two older brothers were away, and my sister lived in a different town. And, of course, he was *the last to use the car when he drove it to the American Legion the previous night*.

Over the years, my dad had been ticketed for drunk driving and had his license suspended twice. I was surprised he didn't kill anyone on the four-mile drive back home each night. Sometimes, Brother 2 or I—once I obtained my driver's license—were summoned to the Legion to drive him home because he was smashed. That was never a good sight to see. My dad in that condition in that godforsaken American Legion. I'll never forget the darkness and the foul, musty odor of that rotten place. Years later, I cannot enter my former hometown or drive by the American Legion without reliving those memories, reopening wounds linked to a time I've tried to erase. It was a place where I was known to some as that skinny kid with an alcoholic father.

In the middle of my freshman year, when I was fifteen, I found myself a job at the one Chinese restaurant in my town, Happy Dragon. After a fifteen-minute interview with the diminutive owner, Yen Wang, I was hired as a dishwasher for minimum wage, which was $2.90 an hour.

My stint in the restaurant business lasted all of ten minutes—five minutes less than it took Yen to interview me for the job. Dishwashing was a mind-numbing experience. I hated it.

I worked in a kitchen hotter than the Sahara desert in summer, wearing an apron and standing amongst a half-dozen men, constantly yelling at each other and me in Cantonese. It was like a bad acid trip. After I washed and cleaned the first tall batch of filthy dishes at breakneck speed on a busy Sunday night when most of Geneva's sizable Jewish population dined there, I untied my apron and handed it to the owner. I waved bye-bye and slinked out the back door.

Owner Yen was screaming at me that I had to *Queen dishes! Queen dishes!* The other Chinese workers barked at me in their native tongue. Once outside, I enjoyed breathing the unsullied air blowing against my face. Freedom. I was sopping wet from sweat. I swear I lost five pounds in those ten minutes of work. I would rather have been jabbed in the eyeballs with knitting needles than work another minute in that hellhole.

I dusted myself off, strolled back to my development, crossed the busy four-lane Route Nine, and ventured to my friend Timmy O'Grady's house. His front door was always unlocked, so I let myself in and plodded up the stairs and into Timmy's bedroom. I found Timmy lying on his bed, his eyes closed and his hands folded across his chest in an X manner, listening to Ted Nugent's "Cat Scratch Fever" blaring from the headphones connected to his stereo. Knowing he was looking for a job, I smacked him on his forehead and told him twice—once when the headphones were on and once when he pulled them off to hear me—that there was a job opening for a dishwasher at the Happy Dragon. He asked me how I knew. I told him it was my job and I quit twenty minutes earlier. Timmy peeled off his headphones, popped up from his messy bed, descended his second-floor stairway, and hopped on his Schwinn ten-speed bicycle to ride to the restaurant I just left. Yen hired him on the spot.

Timmy worked at Happy Dragon for the rest of his high school years, first as a dishwasher, then as a busboy, and then as a waiter, where he made the most money.

Me? I never set foot in Happy Dragon again. However, I did call to have Pu Pu platter, Peking duck, and Moo Shu pork COD orders delivered to my friend Michael Michaels' home on several occasions as pranks. I still remember Happy Dragon's phone number more than forty years later.

Without a doubt, the worst year of my youth was my sophomore year, when I was fifteen. I was miserable and depressed. I spent an entire year without Domonique, the girl I still deeply loved and desperately wanted back. I still sported a grotesque face and an emaciated body. Braces still adorned my teeth, and I had only my guitar as my constant companion. During that period of my youth, TV and film casting agents often approached me to see if I had any acting experience. They wanted to cast me as a monster or zombie since I wouldn't require any makeup. I spent my time brooding, prowling around the neighborhood at night with selected friends, causing mischief, and playing my guitar in our band, The Boys. My father's drinking continued, and I was often the focus of his anger. More than ever that year. I had to be on guard because I never knew when he would erupt in a volcanic fury.

I'd lie in bed at night wide awake, always with a looming fear, anticipating his return home. Then, like clockwork, at 2:11 a.m., I'd hear the sound of keys jingling outside the front door. There would be multiple unsuccessful attempts to unlock it. Racked with anxiety, I'd rise from my bed, walk to the front living room window, slowly pull back the royal blue floor-to-ceiling drapes, and peek out to the front porch. My father would be swaying precipitously in a semi-conscious state. I'd open the door to let him in. When I did, he'd angrily brush past me, mumbling something unintelligible. On cue, my mother descended the thirteen steps to do what she always did—yell and try to reason with him. "Why are you drunk again? This is the fourth night in a row you went to that goddamned American Legion with those lushes you keep company with!" she'd growl, her incisors clenched. "You have a wife and kids at home who need you, blah blah blah."

My dad would look at her with an evil glance from his piercing brown eyes, the same eyes that always paralyzed me into immobility and fear. He'd grunt at my mom and sometimes shove her aside. I'd intervene. That was *my* mother. He'd raise his voice and tell me to mind my own business. Sometimes, he'd get physical with me, and I had to defend myself, backpedaling. He was my father, and I feared him. And physically, he had the upper hand.

He'd slowly make his wobbly way upstairs, holding the railing to steady him, before he'd crash face down on the twin bed in the guest bedroom, clothes on and reeking of cigarettes and beer and American Legion funk. I would plead with my mother then and in the days after to divorce him. I believed if she did, she might find the happiness she deserved with another husband. And, I might find a stepdad who'd show an interest in me. A win-win scenario. Their marriage was floundering and had been for some time. But her love and loyalty to my father were unflinching. While a few friends of mine at the time were praying for their parents to stay together during pending breakups, I prayed for my parents to file for divorce. But my prayers were never answered. My mom was a devout Catholic. And devout Catholics didn't divorce. They stayed married. In good times and in bad, in sickness and in health.

I then begged my mother to at least leave him. But she'd say the same thing—*I'm not leaving; let him leave me*. Even as an immature dum-dum fifteen-year-old, I tried to enlighten my mother that my father had already left her. But that was too abstract for the woman. She didn't get it. My mom was a black-or-white thinker. Gray did not exist in her brain.

I'd then try to reason with my mother, saying if she doesn't leave him, then at least leave him *alone* when he was intoxicated and stumbled in at night—for her safety. My mother could not do it. She must have derived some pleasure from starting arguments with him in the wee morning hours when he was sloshed and angry. It was not a great strategy, nor did it work. She deserved much better.

These interactions were forever seared into my brain. It was then that the seeds were planted not to have children when I got older. I began wondering if I had the same defective gene that would make me emotionally distant and angry and turn me to drink and be away from my wife and children. I'd never know. But if I never had kids, I knew I could never turn my back on them. Or smack them around. I have three siblings. All of them have two children each. I have none. Do the math.

My experiences growing up with my father were vastly different from those of my oldest two siblings. During my formative years, my dad took to drinking. During their formative years, he did not. They remembered a different father who was quiet, present, not angry, engaged, and content with his life. They say timing is everything in life, and my two oldest siblings benefited from that timing.

Just like Elvis had his two versions: the thin Elvis of the 1950s and the bloated drug and alcohol-addicted Elvis of the 1970s, my father also had two versions: the more engaged, non-alcoholic dad of the 1950s and '60s that my two oldest siblings enjoyed, and the drinking dad of the 1970s Brother 2 and I feared. My dad was like Elvis. Brother 2 and I just got the 1970s version.

Not all of my high school experiences consisted of bad grades, angry-drunken dad moments, regrets of lost love, and loneliness in my house. While there was not much to celebrate as a disunited and dysfunctional family growing up with a volatile father as its pack leader, my mother always ensured our Christmases were special. Perhaps it was her way of making up for the insanity of the 364 days preceding Christmas.

I fondly recall the smell of fresh baked Pillsbury cookies wafting through our home assailing my nostrils, our fake tree adorned with ornaments and bright silver tinsel with colorfully wrapped presents underneath, winter scenes decorating our living room, elves on shelves in rooms, garland draped around doorway entrances, and Andy Williams Christmas albums playing from our stereo console record player in our royal blue-carpeted living room. Those were just memories of inside our home. Despite having Muslim, agnostic, Hindu, and Jewish neighbors, most of our development's homes were brightly lit. When there was snow on the ground, it made our neighborhood look like an idyllic winter scene inside a snow globe. Those cherished moments are never lost on me, no matter how young or dumb I was. Watching those stop-motion animated films like *Santa Claus is Comin' to Town*, *The Little Drummer Boy*, *The Year Without a Santa Claus*, and *Rudolph the Red-Nosed Reindeer* televised in the 1960s and '70s always got me excited for the joyous season when people acted nicer to their fellow humans. Then, on January 2nd, they reverted to their nasty behavior toward one another until the following Thanksgiving.

No matter how old I got, I watched those Christmas cartoons every year. My mom made beautiful memories that I enjoyed immeasurably then and look back fondly on now, decades later. For a few years—before he found an extreme interest in girls—Brother 2 and I would sometimes knock on doors in our neighborhood and sing Christmas carols for tip money, receiving a dollar or two per performance. We memorized ten songs and sang them on our neighbors' front porches. After a couple of hours, we'd each have about ten bucks, which was a lot of dough in the early '70s. During the season, I also enjoyed spending time with my friends, riding our Flexible Flyer sleds down snow-packed hills around our development, making snowmen, having snowball fights, playing tackle football in the snow, building igloos, and more. Christmastime was magic.

As it had been during my freshman and sophomore years, I still loved and missed Domonique. Terribly. But there was nothing I could do about the matter. It pained me to see her walking down the hallway holding boyfriend Brandon's hand, kissing or hugging him. He was a friendly, cool kid, so I had no ill feelings towards him. I just hated seeing *them* together. If I wasn't such a dunce and had an ounce of confidence at the time, it could've been me she was loving up on. I foolishly hoped that one day Domonique and Brandon would break up and Domonique and I would reunite. It tore me up to not have her in my life, and I longed for her every day.

Although my awkward appearance and my learning disabilities kept me from trying to find a new girlfriend, I was attracted to a few girls that year. But I had no confidence to approach any of them. And I was not savvy enough to determine if any girl liked me. If one or two did, I would never know; I was that unaware. To deal with my goofy looks, my learning challenges, my drunk and angry dad, and my overall shitty existence at the time, I just kept playing my guitar at home, in my room, alone and sad. My guitar made life more livable when the world around me seemed unbearable.

By sixteen, I was really good on the guitar. My countless hours of self-taught practice paid off. I'd sit on my front porch and strum, with neighborhood kids often stopping by to listen, requesting me to perform songs. I was skilled enough to give guitar lessons to three neighborhood kids a few years younger than me. I charged $8 an hour for private lessons, with each kid coming to my home once a week: two boys, Jared Cohen and Glen Williams, and one girl, Laura Bronski.

Glen was eleven and lived on my block, six houses away. He was a shy kid who seemed to keep deep secrets to himself. Slowly, I pulled him out of his shell so he could communicate with me. In a small way, and over time, I filled the role not just of a guitar teacher but as an older brother/mentor. It was an incredible feeling that I relished. I was able to provide guidance and emotional support to someone younger who needed it. And I embraced the role. Glen was a natural talent who took to the instrument. The kid became almost as good as me within a year. At the one-year mark, Glen's mother informed me that she could no longer afford to pay for his lessons. Times were tough in her household. Because of Glen's unique ability to absorb what I'd taught him and my connection to him, I let her know I'd continue my instruction for free. I did for the next few months before Glen became a far better guitarist than me, and I needed to take lessons from him.

Move the calendar forward fifteen years.

I was out with some friends at a local bar named the Old York Tavern when my friend—a former Marine—tapped me on the shoulder and claimed Axl Rose was checking me out from across the room. I knew the Guns N' Roses frontman had zero chance of being in a local dive bar in Geneva, New Jersey, so I didn't bother to look.

He leaned into me a moment later and said Axl Rose was now staring at me.

My Jarhead buddy was known to instigate trouble for amusement, often looking to pit people against one another to initiate a scrap between them, so I again brushed off his comment. It was Steve just being Steve.

Once again, Steve shouldered me and told me to look. I finally turned to see who he was talking about.

Sure enough, a scruffy-looking guy with long, straight strawberry blond meets red hair, wearing tight black leather pants, a red bandana, black combat boots, and a black leather vest, was staring at me. The guy bore a striking resemblance to the Guns N' Roses singer. Good call. But I informed Steve I had never seen that person in my life, and I wasn't in the mood for a fight.

The Axl lookalike slowly strolled over to me. My ex-Marine friend was in his glory, anticipating a fight. It would make his night, and he would tell the story for decades.

As I squared my shoulders, preparing to throw down inside the blue-collar dive, 'Axl' disarmed me with a simple question: "Are you Mike Kelly?"

I unclenched my balled fist and pulled back to process who this person was.

I answered yes, staring at his face to register him.

'Axl' broke into a broad smile and moved in to hug me, saying he was Glen. *Glen Williams*.

I did a double-take and scanned his face. Yes, it was.

The boy's face was still in there among the long hair and behind the facial scruff. But he was no longer the eleven- or twelve-year-old boy with a crew cut to whom I once gave guitar lessons. He was a grown man in his mid-twenties, with hair down to the middle of his back.

I hugged Glen back—much to the dismay of my ex-Marine buddy Steve—and we stepped to the side to privately chat over a beer.

After exchanging pleasantries and catching up on the old days in the neighborhood, Glen opened up and told me music was his salvation during a bad period in his childhood, a time when his dad was drinking and abusing him.

I had no idea.

Glen said learning how to play the guitar kept him from going down a dark road in life. With a tear welling up in his eyes, my former neighbor placed his hand on my shoulder, looked me square in the eye, and thanked me for teaching him. Glen let me know just how much it meant to him—heavy stuff I was not expecting to hear.

Processing his words, I got choked up, swiping a tear from my eye using the same fist I was prepared to sock him in the face with ten minutes earlier. My emotions composed, I switched gears and asked Glen where he lived and what he was doing for work. Glen said he had an apartment in Hoboken with a few friends, was a musician—*duh*—and played in an original metal band.

He. Was. A. Musician.

Mic drop.

It was rewarding to know I had positively impacted at least one life. It was also a relief to know I hadn't just conducted mischief in my old neighborhood as a kid—I had done some good.

When I was fifteen and a sophomore in high school, I found a job at the regionally famous Englishtown Auction. It was a sprawling outdoor flea market on over fifty acres of unpaved property with five large buildings painted in different colors: blue, green, red, yellow, and brown. Hundreds of vendors flooded the streets to peddle their wares from rickety wooden tables and booths. It was only open on weekends in any weather and was a madhouse when in operation. Up to twenty-five thousand bargain hunters from all over the northeast—NYC, DC, Baltimore, Delaware, Atlantic City, North Jersey, and Southeastern Pennsylvania—would visit on any given weekend day. Picture the movie *Gangs of New York* with all the people and chaos taking place on the unpaved streets. That was the Englishtown Auction on weekends in the 1970s. Complete sensory overload.

In my first job at the Auction, I worked for a street huckster named Noel. He was an inveterate curmudgeon who sold knock-off cassette tapes called *Memex*—a name play on the real Memorex cassette tapes that were wildly popular then. While the authentic tapes cost five dollars per cassette, the nebulously-named Memex tapes were a dollar. People strolling by the tables I was manning would stop in their tracks when they thought they spotted Memorex tapes for such a low price. Their eyes would light up, thinking they were getting a phenomenal bargain. *Memorex tapes for only a dollar each?* they'd ask. My boss Noel stood nearby, his arms crossed, cueing me not to correct them.

Slightly ashamed of myself, I'd nod and enunciate, *Yes,* **Memex** *tapes for a dollar each*. I'd glance back at Noel. He'd nod, then walk away.

After a few weekends of half-heartedly selling those cheap Chinese knock-offs and being unable to sleep at night, I quit. The good news was that I realized I had a conscience—something I had lacked up to that point.

After my brief stint working for snake oil salesman Noel, I found a new job at the Auction working for a better man named Tony Gambino. He was born and raised in Sicily and lived in South Jersey. If Al Capone had a twin brother born forty years later, Tony was him. He was a doppelganger for Scarface, minus the crescent-shaped scar on his dark, chubby cheek.

Tony sold refurbished Pony sneakers and ladies' shoes and operated a small seafood restaurant inside the blue building. It had no tables, just a few bar stools and a counter where you could order your meal. It was always jam-packed as the only place that sold seafood on the entire Auction's vast grounds. I sold his footwear from old tables just outside his smelly seafood shack. When asked where he got the sneakers and shoes, Tony claimed he acquired the rejects directly from the manufacturer for a steep discount, repaired them, and sold them for a profit. Those who knew Tony suggested his products fell off other people's trucks and miraculously landed in Tony's hands. However Tony received his products, I sold them. I asked no questions.

Earning between forty and fifty dollars a day in cash—a small fortune back then—my job was to unpack Tony's white 1978 Ford E350 box truck at 5:30 a.m. every Saturday and Sunday and then hawk as many of his footwear products as possible. If Tony went home with an empty truck at the end of the day, I'd receive a ten-dollar cash bonus.

First, I'd unload all the seafood: 40-lb bags of clams and iced boxes of refrigerated fish. It was nasty. As mentioned earlier, I detested seafood and had a psychological aversion to anything from the ocean. I hated the sight, the smell, and the touch of it. It made me nauseated during that part of the morning. But it was my job to unpack those disgusting products, so I did. I liked Tony and didn't want to let him down.

The seafood took up a third of the truck's cargo compartment. The inner two-thirds contained dozens of large boxes filled with Pony sneakers and ladies' shoes. Once unloaded, the products had to be neatly displayed on the half-dozen dilapidated wood tables Tony rented outside the blue building. Tony's wife, Lucy, newly arrived from Caserta, Italy, didn't speak a lick of English. Yet she and I somehow communicated effectively and worked successfully as a team. Lucy taught me some Italian, and I taught her some English; we got along splendidly.

At the crack of dawn, merchants, vendors, and tour buses flowed in like a slowly creeping tide. By eight o'clock, the flea market was mobbed with thousands of people from all walks of life, an eclectic mix of eager shoppers in a collage of faces in every hue imaginable. Old, young, black, white, Hispanic, other, gay, straight, punk, preppy, poor, wealthy, degenerates, brainiacs, hippies, you name it. They were all Auction shoppers looking for a bargain in the pandemonium. My job was half carnival barker and half salesman. From 7 a.m. until about 4 p.m., I'd shout out with singsong cries of "Ten dollar Pony sneakers and five dollar ladies shoes here! Check 'em out! Pony sneakers here! Ladies shoes here! Come and get 'em while you can. . ." to draw people in.

It worked.

Once lured in, I'd use my prior sales savvy and wheeler-dealer experience in my neighborhood to help a cascade of prospects find what they were looking for and then close each sale. Lucy handled all the money while Tony watched over matters inside his seafood restaurant, puffing his thick cigar in his wide mouth. At day's end, I'd return home hoarse, my throat aching from hours of carnival barking.

I respected and admired Tony. He worked hard and expected others to do the same. When he realized that I worked tirelessly and proved trustworthy and reliable, he took me under his wing and taught me more about life in a few months than my father and three siblings had taught me in my youth. Brown-eyed Tony would sometimes affectionately call me his blue-eyed Irish son. I enjoyed that. At least someone was proud to call me his son.

My Sicilian boss did have a real son named Sal, who sometimes came to work with his dad. Sal was my age and was a super friendly kid, not one of those cocky Italian males who told everyone his family was connected. We worked well together when he showed up, and he became my Auction friend. Sal and I made plans to hang out one day, but we lived an hour away from each other, and neither of us had a driver's license, which made getting together difficult.

Working at the flea market, I learned about sales and marketing. And, of course, about people. It was a master's course on experiential learning: reading behaviors, understanding different cultures and languages, and dealing with adversity, including working in all kinds of weather. The work taught me to become mentally tough and scrappy. In New Jersey, it's called Jersey Tough. Being a grinder to overcome obstacles and succeed in whatever you are doing.

While I appreciated that my mother transported me to and from the Englishtown Auction, I was anxious for the day I could get myself to work. I couldn't wait to turn sixteen to obtain my driver's permit, buy a car, and drive.

CHAPTER 7

A New Me

In 1980, at sixteen, I obtained my New Jersey driver's permit. That allowed me freedom beyond my two feet, thumb, or Huffy bicycle. Desperate to be behind the wheel, I'd solicit anyone to see if they needed me to run errands using our one family car, a recently-purchased 1980 silver-gray Pontiac Lemans. My mom would cringe whenever she'd hand me the keys to practice driving. I'm sure plenty of prayers were recited at church each Sunday to keep me safe. (They worked!)

Later that school year, Brother 1 told me about a car for sale. Someone he knew through his auto body shop was selling a 1966 Volkswagen Beetle with a sunroof and a 4-speed manual shift. It was love at first sight, so I bought it on the spot for $200 cash. As expected, it was in rough condition, but it was affordable. The floorboards were rotted, and I could see the road below in some areas. The rich kids in my hometown proudly drove their brand new Datsun 280ZXs, Triumph TR-7s, Corvettes, and IROCs to school and around town. Though my old Volkswagen lacked the pizzazz of my wealthy classmates' new vehicles, I drove that beat-up Bug just as proudly, shoe-horning as many friends as I possibly could squeeze inside it. My VW made its maiden run with me and four friends just minutes after I bought it. Five young men in one tiny car. It appeared like I was trying to break a world record with human bodies jammed inside. Heads turned, and mouths flew open when five guys wearing varsity jackets spilled out of that little car. Now and then, I'll see an old VW Beetle and peek inside. I can barely fit in the car myself now. I marvel at how I used to transport myself *and* four other guys in it as a teen.

All my friends loved my VW, some dubbing it the Love Bug. However, two of my numbskull buddies decided to prank me by affixing tan masking tape in the number 54 on both of my doors, paying homage to the Disney movie *Herbie the Love Bug*. I was upset once I spied the car in the high school student parking lot. Not because my vehicle was defaced but because they got Herbie's number wrong. The Love Bug was number 53—not 54. As payback, a few days later, both guys were horrified to discover an enormous pile of horse manure sitting on their car seats when they entered their respective clunkers. I drove for weeks sporting that number 54 on my car's doors, then eventually decided to remove the numbers. However, when I peeled off the masking tape, it removed the green paint, thereby still displaying the number 54 on each door. As a fix, I bought black masking tape and replaced what I had removed.

That 1966 Bug was my second favorite car. My all-time favorite was the next one I'd purchase four years later, in 1984. That gem was a 1971 VW Karman Ghia convertible. It was red and had a smashed nose due to an accident by the previous teen owner. I cherished that Karman Ghia and drove it everywhere for two years, mostly with the top down—even in the Northeast winters. It was the coolest car I ever owned.

On Monday, December 8, 1980, I was in my bedroom playing my Gretsch guitar and singing The Beatles' "Across the Universe" before bed. Brother 2 stuck his head into my room and told me John Lennon was shot, then closed the door. Believing he was messing with me, I paid him no mind. What a weird thing for him to say: John Lennon getting shot.

Not more than a minute later, my mother entered my room and told me John Lennon had been shot in Manhattan. She claimed she saw the news report broadcast on the *Monday Night Football* game. In disbelief, I ran upstairs to the TV room to see and hear the news myself.

The game between the Patriots and the Dolphins appeared normal as if nothing unusual had happened. A moment later, the unmistakable nasal voice of ABC know-it-all blowhard broadcaster Howard Cosell reported John Lennon had been shot twice in the back, was rushed to Roosevelt Hospital, and was pronounced dead . . . on . . . arrival.

My jaw dropped.

John Lennon meant a lot more to me than the average Beatles fan. I dedicated countless hours to teaching myself how to play the guitar and other instruments so that I could perform *his* music.

In my school hallways the next morning, I observed several small groups of somber-looking students mourning Lennon's loss. A few invited me to visit the Dakota Building, where John had lived with his wife and young son, to pay tribute to the music icon later that night. But I declined. I was too distraught and did not want to share my deep-rooted feelings with strangers, even if it was to celebrate the life of John Lennon and the incomparable music he had gifted the world. Looking back, forty years later, I realize I should have gone. It's one of my life's regrets.

Certain songs connect to particular moments of my life, and whenever I hear "Across The Universe," I go back to age seventeen, to my small bedroom in Geneva, New Jersey, to that fateful night. While anyone above age twenty seemed old to me as a teenager, John Lennon was only forty when his life was snuffed out. The man had another half of his life to live ahead of him. He was in the process of making a historic comeback with the newly-released *Double Fantasy* album.

Soon after processing the horrific tragedy of the senseless murder committed by a mentally deranged individual, I realized an eerie thing. At the very moments my brother and mother reported to me that John Lennon was shot, I was playing "Across The Universe" on my guitar. That song is considered a 'John song.' (Beatles fans know which songs are John songs, Paul songs, or George songs.) Not only was it a 'John song,' but it was considered one of John's signature songs. Knowing this gave me chills then, as it gives me chills now that I am writing this.

1981 was a good year for me. It was a transformative year, in fact. My braces came off, and—*voila!*—I discovered straight white teeth after seeing nothing but silver for three years. That same year, my face miraculously cleared up. *Poof!* Gone were the annoying pimples scattered about my face. What had previously resembled a topographical map of pepperoni zits was finally clean and smooth. And my voice no longer cracked and danced between octaves. It was deep and done changing. I was no longer repulsed at what I saw staring back in the mirror. That was a relief. Girls who previously turned their heads away from me in disgust as if they just smelled rotten eggs now turned towards me to smile. As you can imagine, my confidence rose to an all-time high. I still hung out with my best friends Anthony, Mehmet, Bobby, and Patrick. We went bowling at night, to the beach on weekends, and drove all over town in our cars. I had my Bug, Mehmet had a brand new Trans Am, and Anthony bought a 1968 Chrysler Newport. It was enormous! You could fit my VW Bug in his back seat alone. We'd comfortably accommodate eight or nine kids in there at times. Seriously. Although Anthony was a terrible driver, everyone loved him and hopped in his big boat for what they'd expect to be a nice ride from such a calm kid. Soon into their ride, they experienced the most terrifying moment of their lives. While a peaceful and quiet young man, Anthony drove like a maniac. He made hairpin turns and disregarded speed limits, stop signs, traffic lights, and pedestrians crossing at walkways. It was like an angry blind man was operating the vehicle. Miraculously, he never got into an accident. The man-child was lucky.

While bowling one night with my friends at Howell Lanes, about ten miles south of my hometown, I bumped into a pretty girl—literally—standing in the lane next to me with three of her friends. Anthony shoved me with his male Silverback gorilla strength, shouting, "I LOVE YOU!" I flew about eight feet across my lane into hers and slammed into the poor girl. It was not the best way to meet someone.

Blushing and trying to recover from the sudden situation I was thrust into, I fumbled along to apologize and then struck up a conversation with the bewildered beauty.

Maria was her name. She was my age, lived in Howell, two towns south of my hometown, off Route Nine, and was a junior like me. She was pretty and bore a striking resemblance to Domonique, with whom I was still in love. Maria had dark, almost black hair and brown eyes, stood five-five, and had a shapely mouth full of straight white teeth. We dated several times, but things fizzled out after a month.

Our dates consisted of me driving to her home, sitting on her living room couch, and watching TV—all while her protective parents took turns poking their heads into the room every few minutes to make sure I was not having sex with their daughter. After a month, Maria stopped answering my phone calls. I was disappointed, but I didn't blame her. I had no game and was unskilled in such matters. I didn't know what to do with her or how to date. I was boring. After Maria dumped me, I realized I should've taken her out for dinner, ice skating, roller skating, bowling at the place we met, to a movie, or driven her to the beach to watch the waves rush in and out. There were a dozen other places I could have taken her, places I'd eventually take girls once I developed more confidence and expanded my knowledge base. And, of course, once I made more money. But that's where my older brothers' advice would have come in handy. "Hey, Mike, this is what I recommend you do with Maria. Go to (fill in the name of a place). It's cool, and she'll love it." Or "Why don't we double date? You and Maria can join me and my girlfriend to (fill in the name of a restaurant or pizza parlor)." Surely, that would have scored big points with Maria and kept her interested in me. My older brothers could have easily shared advice from their successful experiences with girls. Both were knowledgeable on the subject. And I had great reverence for them. If either suggested I jump off a cliff, I'd be thrilled with the attention and would have considered doing so. So, I would take their guidance on girls.

My oldest brother was once a New Jersey state long jump champion in high school and a nationally-ranked track star in the high hurdles and long jump. (White men can jump!) As an auto body business owner and talented artist bursting with creativity, he created the coolest car in town: his customized candy apple red 1972 VW Bug. It was admired everywhere he drove it. Brother 1 covered the rear side windows with Bondo and painted over both sides with Michelangelo's famous Creation of Adam (a.k.a. God Touches Man) scene from the Sistine Chapel ceiling. The car was worthy of gracing the cover of auto magazines. He was a handsome devil with a killer mustache. And girls loved him.

Brother 2—the model—was also a handsome devil with dark hair and eyes. He was a go-with-the-flow kind of guy whose accolades in youth sports could fill a phone book. Girls lined up at our home wanting to date him.

Both my brothers had game. Lots of it. They enjoyed female suitors swooning over them, and I marveled at how easily they talked to the opposite gender. They could turn confident, beautiful young ladies into awkward and unsure teen girls. It was remarkable. Yet they didn't provide any pointers or share their knowledge to help me with my lack of understanding of girls. I had to figure things out for myself, which sucked. It would be like having NBA legends Michael Jordan and Larry Bird as your brothers, but you would have to teach yourself how to play basketball because they had no interest in teaching you.

In my junior year, I joined the high school track team. Not wanting to run or jump, I decided to throw the javelin instead. I had a strong arm, good throwing mechanics, and experience around my neighborhood tossing things (rocks, footballs, baseballs, eggs, snowballs, firecrackers, etc.). So, I thought I'd put that experience to use to do something productive. I was still skinny; my body resembled a javelin, which was ironic. It'd be like a short, fat, round guy becoming a bowler. My presence drew snickers from some stocky opponents. I'd get looks like *This bony kid is competing against me? I'm going to crush him!* The funny thing is, eight times out of ten, I'd beat those guys in meets, throwing ten or twenty feet farther than them. I even beat the muscle-heads built to look like they could toss that spear to the moon. In my case, looks were deceiving. What I lacked in size I made up for in technique and determination.

Junior year brought me an additional friend named Richie Rosetti. Richie was a three-sport athlete at Geneva High School—football, wrestling, and baseball—and was voted best-looking by our school's yearbook committee. He was a kind and generous kid without ego and another Italian boy who resembled a full-grown man. All the girls liked him, and all the guys wanted to hang with him. And I was one of the fortunate few who did.

Though I had competed in youth football with Richie since age eight and played with him on the freshman football team, we never hung out until our junior year. Mehmet was tight with Richie and re-acquainted me with him. My core four friends at this time were Mehmet, Anthony, Richie, and Bobby. My cerebral friend, Patrick, defected from the group during junior year and began spending time with kids who would go on to attend Yale, Princeton, and other elite universities. He made the right decision, breaking away from us hooligans. We were not going to help get him into college, that's for sure. We understood the situation and wished him well. It's what he needed to do to stay on his life path.

While most of my friends and I were driving beat-up jalopies with dented fenders, ripped interiors, different color quarter panels, and duct tape holding parts together, Richie drove a brand new powder blue 1981 Ford Thunderbird, courtesy of his dad, who gifted it to Richie for his seventeenth birthday. It was a beautiful, sleek machine with electric windows, air conditioning, and a computerized digital dashboard and speedometer—the first I'd seen. It was the fanciest car I'd been in and much nicer than any of our parents' cars. While we never asked, we all wondered what Richie's father did for a living.

Richie's older brother attended Glassboro State College in South Jersey and played on the rugby team he formed. On an occasional Friday after school, Richie, Anthony, Mehmet, and I would drive down to Glassboro for the weekend to play scrimmages with his team. Our crew gave them a practice squad against which to sharpen their skills for future college competition. Anthony was fast as lightning and hit like a truck, Richie and Mehmet were both sturdily built and tough as nails, and I was quick and a good tackler, so we made a formidable practice crew. As a bonus at nighttime—after getting our asses kicked on the rugby field by grown men during the day—we got to experience a taste of college nightlife. It was an eye-opening adventure of drinking, rituals, and sex—not for us high schoolers, but for the college guys. We were just bystanders.

When not driving to Glassboro, we often day-tripped down to Atlantic City, usually in Anthony's car, since it could comfortably hold eight of us. We loved going to Atlantic City. Richie was a talented poker player who also dabbled in roulette. He'd bring a wad of cash on our trips compared to the ten or twenty bucks the rest of us would have. While lint, a few coins, and crumpled singles came out of my pocket, fifty and hundred dollar bills flew out of Richie's pockets. Richie sat at poker and roulette tables next to people double, triple, and quadruple his age. The rest of us played the slot machines until we lost all our money, which usually took five to fifteen minutes. But we didn't care. Richie would always gladly hand us a ten- or twenty-dollar bill to keep playing with no strings attached. We were thrilled to be inside the AC casinos where everything was happening.

One day, I met former heavyweight boxing title challenger Chuck "The Bayonne Bleeder" Wepner at Harrah's

Casino. He was a Goliath of a man best known for going 15 rounds in a title fight against Muhammad Ali. That legendary battle inspired the Oscar-winning film *Rocky*.

Unfortunately, not all our experiences in the gambling resort town beside the sea were pleasant ones.

One day, while driving down to AC in Richie's new Ford Thunderbird, we were pulled over by two New Jersey State Police cruisers and a New Jersey State Police helicopter. *Hmm. Perhaps payback for the New Jersey State Police candy bar scam I perpetrated with my friend Michael eight years before?*

Oblivious because we were listening to music, jabbering, and joshing each other, we thought the cops were following someone else. That was until the police cruisers surrounded Richie's vehicle. At the same time, we saw the helicopter hovering directly above Richie's T-bird. They meant business. That's when we first soiled our pants.

With an equal mix of confusion and fright, Richie pulled over and parked on the shoulder. Travelers on the southbound lanes of the Garden State Parkway crawled to check out the developing scene. Irritated troopers dressed in tactical gear and armed with high-powered assault weapons leaped out from their cruisers. They pointed their guns at us and barked commands for us to get out of the car slowly with our hands up, or they'd shoot. Everything was happening so quickly. Second soiling for us kids.

Completely bewildered, we cautiously exited Richie's vehicle and got down on the hot pavement as instructed, face down, and spread eagle, the macadam burning our faces and bodies from the blistering sun. The state troopers handcuffed us as our faces pressed against the scorching pavement. Then they angrily searched Richie's T-Bird. Richie momentarily lifted his head and questioned why they were messing up his new car. Two troopers turned and pointed their rifles at him, firing obscenities at the teen. These guys were pissed off. The stains from our respective pants grew larger.

After a frantic and harrowing ten minutes, the stone-faced troopers ordered us to sit up and unlocked us from the handcuffs. Trembling, we stood up and surveyed each other's crotches to see which had the most prominent soil mark. One trooper broke his silence and informed us there was a bank robbery in nearby Tuckerton. A getaway car with a group of black males in it matching Richie's car was reported driving south on the Parkway. I piped up and pointed out that we were a group of *white* males. The trooper shot me a dirty look. I shut my mouth and placed my head down.

The troopers told us we were free to go without apologizing. Within ten seconds, the state troopers' cars disappeared into the Garden State Parkway traffic, and the New Jersey State Police helicopter disappeared into the sky. The soiled marks on our pants remained much longer.

At the beginning of track season in March, when I was a junior, I took notice of a cute girl named Miranda O'Connor. She was a mile runner on the girls' team who had thick red hair, milky white skin, and a great pair of athletic legs as long as I was tall. Miranda liked me, and although I was still head-over-heels in love with Domonique, I had a bit of a crush on Miranda. As junior prom neared, Miranda's friends began questioning who I was taking. I wasn't even thinking about prom. I knew Domonique would be going with her boyfriend of two years—the same opportunistic kid who swooped in a few days after I broke up with Domonique the first week into our freshman year. I didn't know if I would even attend.

As the days passed, Miranda's friends told me she wanted me to ask her to prom and urged me to ask their friend. It seemed like a good idea, so I did. And Miranda cheerfully accepted. All was good—until I messed things up.

A girl I liked more named Diane Macaluso—whom I thought would never like me in a hundred years—caught wind I was taking Miranda. Seizing upon that information, Diane made it known *she liked me* and wanted me to take her to prom. Within a couple of days, I went from having zero girls show an interest in me to having two girls wanting me to take them to junior prom. I was flattered, yet confused. Diane's friends, whom I'd never talked to, came out of the woodwork and lobbied me to take their friend. Diane was a sophomore, but my grade often dated down a grade or two because we were typical immature boys. If we were to match up with our emotionally mature peers, we'd have to ask first-grade girls to prom. I'm not sure school officials would allow that.

So there I was. For two years, my Gretsch guitar had been my girlfriend. Now, not one but two attractive young ladies wanted to go to the prom with me. My head was spinning.

Because I had disengaged older brothers who showed no interest in me, a father who spent more awake hours drinking at the American Legion than he did at home, and a mother consumed with her husband's alcoholism and dealing with issues resulting from his predicament, I could not get advice on how to handle the situation. I did not know what to do. And because I was a boy of paralyzing stupidity at times, I asked Diane to prom, too. After Diane accepted, I quickly realized that my prom dates would soon find out about each other. *I couldn't go with two girls, could I?* Only famous people could pull that off. But an unfamous, dopey high school kid? Impossible.

This dilemma weighed heavily on my skinny shoulders. I liked Diane and was thrilled she even knew who I was, let alone showed an interest in me. She was popular and cute as hell and caught the eye of many boys. But Miranda was also cute, sweet, intelligent, and had a great body. Plus, in fairness to Miranda, she liked me first, and I asked her to prom first. And she accepted first. It should have been her.

To further complicate matters, a friend of mine, a wrestling stud built like a Greek god who'd just won a New Jersey State wrestling championship—the first in my high school's history—told me he liked Diane Macaluso and was going to ask her to prom if I didn't. That new information swayed my decision and swung the pendulum in Diane's direction. *Would Diane still like me after she had a chance to get to know Mr. New Jersey State Wrestling Champ?* I highly doubted it. So, I became territorial and acted quickly.

My heart thumping like a bass drum, I called Miranda on the phone to break the bad news to her. It was the most unpleasant, awkward thing I'd ever done. And that was coming from a kid who once dressed in a long black cassock and conducted bogus religious ceremonies off a busy road in front of a crowd of people and ran around bare-assed on a basketball court in front of spectators in a school gymnasium. Before I could do my dirty work, Miranda excitedly told me about the dress she had just bought and how pretty it was. Then she told me that she made me a present and couldn't wait for us to start dating, blah blah blah. She was giddy.

Fuuuuuck! I thought, tightening my grip on the phone's receiver.

Umm . . . yeah . . . ahh . . . about the prom . . .

Cringing, I told Miranda I had also asked Diane to prom and ultimately decided to go with her instead.

Silence on her end of the line.

I apologized repeatedly.

Continued silence on her end.

It was an incredibly uncomfortable moment, and I felt horrible—like I was going to burn in hell for eternity horrible. Then I heard Miranda cry. Though I didn't think it could be possible, I felt even worse. I kept apologizing, but Miranda hung up after my fourth or fifth apology. I wanted to hide in a cave somewhere far away.

Miranda spoke not a single word to me for the remainder of my junior year and the next school year—our senior year. The girl didn't even *look* at me. Neither did her friends, all of whom were on the girls' track team. Not only did I see them in my classes, but I also saw them during track practice and at meets. Uncomfortable is an understatement.

After a few weeks, I crafted an apology letter and slipped it into Miranda's locker.

It went unanswered.

Why did I make yet another terrible decision—one that hurt another girl's feelings? What was wrong with me? I honestly didn't know. Maybe I did have rocks in my head like my father often told me.

I didn't blame Miranda for wanting nothing to do with me. She felt spurned and tricked. I would have felt the same way. For twenty-plus years, this unkind act gnawed away at me. Somehow, I was determined to right my past wrong, if only a little.

At my twenty-year high school reunion, with my wife at my side, I cautiously approached Miranda and apologized to her again. I let her know I still felt horrible about what I did as a senseless teenager two decades earlier. Her husband at her side, Miranda graciously accepted my apology, and we hugged.

I still feel terrible for having hurt Miranda O'Connor back then. She was a sweet girl, a good girl. Not a partyer, not a skank, not a troublemaker. What an incompetent dumbass I was. And mean.

I deserved what I got when I decided to date Diane over Miranda. I'd soon find out Diane was a wolf in sheep's clothing who turned out to be as honest and faithful as Bill Clinton.

Karma.

D

Diane Macaluso was exceptionally cute. Five-two, with a curvy body, long brown hair, pouty full lips, a nice smile, and trusting big brown eyes. Cheerleader. Witty. Hung out with the popular girls and had all the right stuff that teenage boys would fantasize about. But I soon realized after dating Diane that there was another side to her. A dark side. The girl was a player. The revelation came to me slowly, then in a tidal wave. I brushed off the reports and gave her the benefit of each doubt. *People were just jealous*, I thought. Her trusting eyes and ability to expertly manipulate my emotions tricked me into thinking she liked only me. But more and more people confirmed the cheating reports, though I could not discern if they were true. They were not just vague rumors but multiple eyewitness accounts shared by credible people. After it all became too much, I approached Diane one day and questioned her about a few specific instances and if the news was accurate. She rolled her big brown puppy dog eyes, blinking those long, thick eyelashes, and denied everything. Diane claimed the boys were just friends, and they were all hanging out together. Nothing to worry about. Then she asked who told me she was cheating. Like an idiot, I named names. And then Diane began attacking that person's character, saying that they were a liar and a loser. And I believed her.

But the seeds of paranoia were planted in my brain. It messed me up. Big time.

D

To help me deal with all the pent-up frustration of dating a reported serial cheater and not understanding why I didn't have the power or courage to break up with Diane, I focused on my guitar work and playing in my town's recreational basketball league. The Boys had broken up because Anthony became inseparable from his new girlfriend Cathy, a junior attending a different high school. The Boys would have band practice, and Cathy would always show up. Like me, Anthony had significant attention deficits to begin with, and whatever morsel of attention he had to offer was spent on Cathy. Which meant he had none left for the band. We'd be rehearsing a song, and Anthony and Cathy would lovingly eyeball each other. In mid-song, Anthony would place his guitar down and start making out with Cathy. *Anthony!* I'd bark. *Get back on the guitar and sing the damn song we're in the middle of. Make out with her after practice!*

Well-intended wishes, but it never happened. Cathy rarely left Anthony's side. She was Chang to his Eng, attached at the breastbone. Our band was no match for Anthony's raging hormones. As such, The Boys broke up. My dreams of becoming a rock star were thwarted. Kaput. Disappeared in a puff of smoke. Just like that.

Thanks, Yoko!

Upset at Anthony and his girlfriend, I decided to give them payback for their part in breaking up The Boys. I called Cathy and told her I caught Anthony making out with another girl in my school. That was a lie, but the seed was planted. Cathy believed me. The damage was done. Later that evening,

Diane and I were watching MTV at her home. It was one of the rare moments we were not fighting. Soon into that temporary bliss, Diane's mother poked her head into the room and informed me that my friend was at the front door and wanted to see me. I gulped and asked who it was. She said a boy named Anthony.

My eyes grew large.

I scanned the TV room for a place to hide. Nothing. Next, I thought of an escape route. Could I sneak out the back door? Or climb out the first-floor bedroom window? I could run. But even though I was fast, Anthony was faster. He'd catch me in a few seconds. So, I decided my only option was to deal with the mess I created and answer the call.

When I sheepishly approached the front door, I peered through the glass louvers and noticed a look on Anthony's face that I had never seen before. He. Was. Livid.

Gone was the ever-present goofy grin and relaxed muscled body. Anthony was standing in a fighting posture, his muscles bulging, the veins in his neck and forehead pulsing. *What did I get myself into?*

I drew in my breath and opened the door. When I did, Anthony bellowed, "WHAT DID YOU TELL CATHY?"

I slipped outside onto the front porch, closed the door behind me, fessed up, told him the truth, why I did it, apologized, and hugged him.

Surprisingly, Anthony returned to his usual calm and happy self almost immediately after my confessional apology and hug. He started laughing. A warm wave of relief flowed through me. We were good.

Whew!

Since there was no more band, sports it was. Though I was built like a javelin, I was among the top javelin throwers in the Jersey Shore Conference. As mentioned, I liked to throw things: footballs, snowballs, eggs, rocks, baseballs, etc. As it turned out, I was also pretty good at throwing javelins. In competition, I'd get three tosses to score team points. I didn't have to run a mile around the track or pole vault twelve feet up in the air and hope I'd land on the pad on my way down to avoid breaking my spinal cord, and I didn't have to scrape my bony shins on splintered wooden hurdles as I ran over them. The javelin suited me just fine. I received positive attention from coaches and classmates during that time, just not from Miranda on the girls' track team. She was still pissed that I unasked her to prom.

    That positive attention made up for the self-esteem I was losing going out with a reported serial cheater. Dating Diane crushed my psyche. I'd think I was all cool, throwing the javelin and winning competitions, playing the guitar, and wearing my varsity jacket around town with friends greeting me and patting me on the back in the high school hallways. The next day, I was questioning my girlfriend at her locker if it was true she had sex with another boy at a party the night before, as reported by multiple sources. All my built-up confidence and self-esteem were destroyed when that happened. It was emasculating. I wouldn't wish a cheater on anyone. It's why I never became one myself.

CHAPTER 8

Your Cheating Heart

My father and I barely spoke during my senior year of high school. I steered clear of him, which wasn't easy to do. He was unemployed and had been for more than two years. He was home during the day and anchored himself at the dining room table, devising mathematical formulas to win the lottery. My father was a skilled mathematician who loved solving numbers problems. He preferred numbers over human attention and communication—especially from his family members. Within a fourteen-month period, he won the lottery twice—the Pick 4 lotteries, not the Pick 6 ones that had the big money payouts. He first won $1,800 in 1980—today's equivalent of $5,000. Then, in 1981, he won $4,000—today's equivalent of $11,500. The money helped pay bills and buy my parents a new 1980 Pontiac Lemans and Brother 2 a new white 1981 Dodge Omni 024. Those winnings had convinced my father that more was to come.

With the most awkward ages of my younger teen years behind me, my relationship with my mother began to improve when I was seventeen. Even though I knew my mother still believed I was a moron due to my low grades in school, my mom always had my back. No doubt I loved her a ton, but I began respecting her and saw her in a new light in my later teen years.

At that time, my mother was in her mid-fifties, and as a temporary outlet to let off steam built up from her stressful life at home, she began playing tennis. The woman never took a single lesson but became a vicious player. My mom competed with and most often beat women ten or twenty years younger than her who'd been taking lessons for years—neighborhood ladies, homemakers from other developments, and wealthy wives of VIP businessmen who paid for their spouse's private instruction. They all fell to my mom. Until then, I used to think my athletic abilities came from my father. Maybe not.

If sophomore year was my worst year in high school, then senior year was my best. My serial-cheating girlfriend aside, I was enveloped in pure happiness. I played basketball in my hometown's recreation league and won a championship that year, drove around town with friends in my VW Bug, improved upon my guitar playing, and added some new friends. Some buddies used to jokingly call me United Nations because I was friendly with all kinds of kids in school, not just members of my clique. I was like a Venn Diagram, overlapping with other circled sets. I'd talk to the burnouts, drama club kids, jocks, musicians, freshmen, nerds, farmers, special eddies, Goths, minority kids, and everyone in between of all grades.

I wished things were as good with my girlfriend as they were with my social life. Diane and I had been dating for a year at that point, and the stories of her infidelity continued to flood in. I was devastated hearing them. I believed Diane was going to be my wife one day. But, like the song lyrics, I was a fool in love.

Over my senior year, our relationship worked like this: Diane would cheat on me—kiss, make out with, or have sex with another guy—I'd find out from someone other than my girlfriend, I'd confront her about the reports, she'd vehemently deny them, I'd catch her in a lie—or three—she'd eventually confess, cry, blink those big brown doe eyes, convincingly tell me she made a mistake, was sorry, and loved only me. I'd bury my face in my hands, and she'd grovel up to me over the ensuing days and swear it would never happen again. And I believed her.

That girl cast a wicked spell on me. And like a moron, I took her back. Every. Single. Time.

I think it was because in between her episodes of cheating, she was kind, loving, and affectionate to me. The many low points were offset by moments of physical joy that we experienced together. But the process was mentally and emotionally exhausting. Even though I was a year older and a grade above Diane, I remained naive and unskilled in handling such relationship matters. As a result, Diane was a grand maestro and played me like a fiddle.

My only experiences with girls before Diane had been positive ones. Mandy was a sweetheart. We never disagreed, let alone quarreled, and I never noticed a wandering eye with her—despite the fact that there were always a dozen boys of all ages buzzing around Mandy's home on any given day. And I never caught her in a lie, let alone twenty different lies. We only stopped seeing each other because we attended separate schools in various towns and had extracurricular activities that kept us apart.

And Domonique was an angel: compassionate, loving, trusting, and many other wonderful things. She wouldn't hurt a fly, let alone her boyfriend's feelings. We broke up because I was a dumb-ass and made a life-altering mistake by running from her, believing she'd eventually break up with me due to my unappealing features and immaturity at the onset of puberty.

But Diane was cut from a different cloth. Enduring her episodes of infidelity, all I kept thinking was that *Domonique would never mistreat me*. Domonique never cheated on me when we dated, and she never cheated on her boyfriend during three years of dating him. She was a loyal girl. I knew because I kept tabs on her from afar. Every guy adored Domonique, and most wanted to date her, with some trying to. But she never strayed from her boyfriend. Ever.

I was emotionally fragile and vulnerable. I needed a girlfriend to help build my confidence and encourage me since I wasn't getting that at home. Diane knew that. I had trust issues with my father, who'd be quiet one moment and then explode in a drunken rage and attack me the next. Diane knew that. I needed to be able to trust the people closest to me. Most of all, my girlfriend. Diane knew that. But she didn't care. To be able to exploit that vulnerability was something I could never do to anyone, let alone someone I deeply cared about.

Amazingly, despite Diane's ongoing infidelity, I never cheated on her, though I had several opportunities to do so. Even though I was a somewhat goofy-looking kid, other girls liked me and made it known that they wanted to date me. But I always resisted temptation and stayed loyal to my girlfriend. Imagine that? I'd refuse a make-out session—or more—with pretty or sexy girls, telling them I was dating Diane and didn't cheat. The astonished girls would remind me that my girlfriend was caught making out with—or more—another guy at a party the night or week before. Everybody thought I was nuts, including me. I honestly didn't know why I stayed with Diane Macaluso. The girl made me look like a complete fool and crushed whatever pride, self-esteem, and confidence I had developed through sports, music, and friendship over the past two years. My friends, their parents, mutual acquaintances—even a handful of her friends who felt bad for me—urged me to break up with her. They let me know she was a player. But I didn't listen. I kept taking Diane back and forgiving her, thinking she'd be faithful the next time. But Diane was who she was—a serial cheater. And I was who I was—a moronic dope in love with her. Due to her two-timing ways, I could no longer trust the girl. It was terrible energy, and I carried it around with me each day. Every moment when I was not with the girl, I thought she was cheating on me. It was the worst feeling, distrusting a loved one like that. I'd never experienced that emotion toward a girlfriend before, yet I could not break up with Diane. She had some crazy hold on my heart. Then it dawned on me. I realized I was like my mother, the enabler willing to be mistreated. And Diane was like my father, the continued emotional abuser I couldn't leave. The similarities were striking.

After dating Diane for a year, not only did I discover she had a wandering eye and acted upon it, but she was also mean to others. She constantly disparagingly gossiped about her friends behind their backs and was ruthless toward her younger sister. Diane was also belligerent and aggressive to her parents, often making flippant remarks or cursing at them during conversations. I'm not sure why she was so mean and moody, but she certainly had a lot of venom for her family. She would say the most vicious things to her kid sister, who looked up to her. Diane would sneer at her younger sibling and, with theatrical flamboyance, constantly call her a disgusting fat cow and tell her no boy would ever want to date her because she was *fugly*. It was brutal. I'd cringe and ask her to stop. It was like watching a baby seal being clubbed over its head. Diane's little sister would burst into tears and bolt out of the room, hysterical. Unfazed, Diane would flash a devilish grin, knowing her hurtful words struck the bullseye to her sister's heart. And then she'd start laughing maniacally. I'd stare blankly at her, shaking my head, thinking I was dating a madwoman, a psychopath. Sometimes, I'd go into her kid sister's room and console her while she was sulking, letting her know Diane was also mean to me, too, if it made her feel any better. (It didn't). As a fellow youngest sibling, I felt for the kid. But there was nothing I could do to help her.

    Diane would also rail against her mother, a tiny older lady born in Europe who spoke with a thick accent. I couldn't believe a daughter could say such horrible things to her mother, but Diane did just that. Quite often, actually. It was staggering. I'd wince and slowly back out of the room whenever she would go on a tirade. It was so uncomfortable for me. Not for Diane, though. She reveled in dispensing nastiness to those closest to her. I could never say anything like that to my mother. What the hell was the matter with me? Why couldn't I just dump this crazy chick? Practically everyone gave me the memo to do just that. But I just kept crumpling up the memo and tossing it back to the people who handed it to me, saying I loved Diane. Maybe it was cosmic payback—karma coming back to haunt me due to mishandling the Miranda situation by not taking her to my junior prom after I asked her and instead taking Diane. Or breaking up with Domonique by using someone else to do my dirty work a few years before. Who knew? I sure as hell didn't.

To flee from my ongoing woes with Diane Macaluso, I would escape Geneva. Somehow, a new friend acquired free tickets to a club called The Underground in New York City, located in the Union Square neighborhood. A dozen buddies would pile into a couple of cars and brave the gridlocked traffic through the Holland Tunnel and Manhattan. After spending too much time searching for available parking spaces on the streets, we'd park anywhere, not caring about the inevitable parking tickets, and finally enter the dance club. Once inside, we'd plunge into the surging crowds and enjoy an authentic nightclub experience in Manhattan on a Friday or Saturday night. While most of our peers met at hometown pizza joints or the local mall to hang out, my friends and I were in New York City. We felt important. Whereas I used to obtain drinks for free at home or friends' homes, I quickly discovered that drinks out at bars cost money. A lot of money. We'd spend $4 for Diet Cokes, $6 for bottles of beer, and $10 for mixed drinks (1982 prices, mind you), along with overpriced food. Then we'd have to fend off the attractive rose girls strolling about the club and persistently pressuring you to buy a $5 rose for any female patron standing next to you. Despite the parking nightmares and costly expenses, we traveled to The Underground a handful of times and felt like adults. It was empowering being a Jersey teen hanging out in Manhattan.

When not visiting The Underground, my extended group of friends—which had included Joel Edwards, Dave Stein, Joe Cirone, Paul Schmidt, and Gerard Bizzetti—continued to venture down to Glassboro State College on some weekends to compete in rugby scrimmages. Afterward, we'd attend the college's various parties. In addition to the ventures to Glassboro State College, Anthony, Richie, Mehmet, Bobby, and I continued our trips to AC to mostly watch Richie and Mehmet gamble. After my measly $20 ran out—usually in about eight minutes—I'd walk the historic boardwalk, cozy up to a blackjack table pretending to play so I could score free drinks from the scantily clad cocktail waitresses walking about in stilettos, or wander about in the other boardwalk casinos. Afterward, in the wee hours of the morning, when Richie's money would eventually disappear, we'd drive to a 24-hour Jersey diner and stuff our faces with comfort food. That's where Richie and Mehmet would talk about what they could've, would've, and should've done differently with their gambling performances.

    On a few occasions during my senior year, after school, my friends and I would drive to Manasquan Beach, enjoying what the Jersey Shore had to offer. I'd play my guitar on the beach, entertaining small crowds circled around me, nodding their heads and singing the words to the songs I performed. Anthony would remove his shirt and display his chiseled olive-colored physique, and the girls would flock to him like moths to a bright light. Standing next to Anthony, I looked like the before photo in the advertisements for weight-training products, while Anthony looked like the after pic. We enjoyed good times during the days when Jersey beaches were not as overpriced and overcrowded as they are today.

    At the end of my senior year, on some Saturday nights when my girlfriend and I were fighting, Mehmet and I took turns visiting Club Xanadu or the Stone Pony in Asbury Park, a block from each other and the boardwalk. Because I was eighteen—the legal drinking age in New Jersey in 1982—and because Mehmet used his lookalike older brother's driver's license as a fake ID, we were admitted and enjoyed watching cover bands perform live music, girls dancing and pretending to be people we were not just to clown around. Mehmet would say his name was Vinnie, I'd say my name was Joe, and by the night's end, we had no idea what our names were when talking to people. We were just as confused as they were.

    Aside from the good times I experienced hanging out with my friends, I began thinking about my post-high school plans for the first time in my life. While most of my buddies had already applied to and had been accepted into colleges, I hadn't given thought to my future, academically or otherwise.

Still beset by my undiagnosed learning disabilities, I was struggling just to graduate high school. The last thing I was thinking about was continuing my education at a higher level. I wanted a break from school. I'd been a part of it for twelve years. The first seven were all good—primarily As and a few Bs. The last five years not so good. College was pushed, and I was brainwashed to believe I needed a degree to earn a nice living one day. But I questioned that. Both my parents had college degrees. Yet my dad had been unemployed for most of my high school years, and my mother was a stay-at-home mom who babysat a few neighborhood kids three days a week, earning little more than minimum wage. Where were the great jobs and good earnings resulting from their education?

On the flip side, my oldest brother dropped out of college and made a lot of money running his auto body business. I also noticed kids a couple of years older than me operating their lawn-cutting businesses and making tons of cash. These guys were driving fancy cars, wearing the latest clothes, and had girls on each arm when about town. So, I wasn't entirely sold on college. But I also wasn't sure what I wanted for a career. My interest in becoming a professional musician faded when The Boys broke up. However, I considered working in a music studio, helping artists record albums. Possibly a sound engineer or assistant record producer. I had an exceptional ear for music, as I'd taught myself to play multiple instruments just by listening to songs. I didn't need to take lessons. I wasn't sure how to become a sound engineer or record producer in the music industry. I wanted to discover how, so I stopped into my high school guidance counselor's office one day to learn the specifics.

Mr. Brunson was an older black man with a bald top part of his head, yet with afros sprouted on the sides of his head over each of his ears. He looked like a black Bozo the

Clown. Known to bend an elbow, Mr. Brunson carried a flask inside his jacket pocket and had bloodshot eyes and a perpetual grin on his dark, chubby face. Being appointed to the academically challenged, bottom-tier, directionless kids like me, I couldn't blame him for carrying a flask. If I had to counsel kids like me, I'd carry *two* flasks—one in each interior jacket pocket.

I spent a few minutes expressing my passion for music to Mr. Brunson, informing him of my self-taught ability to play multiple instruments and exceptional ear for music and how I wanted to parlay those gifts into a career in the music industry as a recording or sound engineer or perhaps work at one of the big studios where famous artists record their music. Halfway through my narrative, Mr. Brunson's eyes began to close. I faked a cough to wake him up temporarily, then asked him what colleges taught sound engineering or music recording. Mr. Brunson smiled and told me to go to college, then stood up from his chair and thanked me for coming in. Dumbfounded, I stared at him. He continued smiling yet said nothing further. I turned and shuffled out of his office.

What prudent advice. Bravo!

I relayed the above story to my mother, and she was disappointed. I believe she called the school's principal to inform him of Mr. Brunson's lack of guidance in his guidance counselor position.

Since my mom was preoccupied with my father's drinking, she wasn't able to provide the proper guidance and support I needed at the time. She was limited. But my mom always took the time to listen to me perform a song or two, which I always appreciated. It showed she cared. On the other hand, my father had zero interest in my musical abilities or in listening to me play any instrument. He couldn't care less. Wanting to assist in my career planning, my mother offered the best help she could.

Although I'd taught myself how to play six instruments—guitar, bass, harmonica, piano, tambourine, and recorder—my mother was oblivious to my musical abilities. She lacked a keen sense of the obvious. As a result, she suggested I take a vocational aptitude test.

Huh?

That was amazing.

It would be like a mother *not* suggesting her chainsaw-juggling son become a circus performer. Or, like a mother whose exceptionally tall son was lightning quick, had superior leaping abilities, and could do fancy slam dunks while playing basketball, wondering what her son's skills were.

Bless her heart, my mother.

Because her eyes were primarily focused on my alcoholic father, she was unable to see me, her son, right before her. So my mom found some self-proclaimed vocational expert named Marv Davis in the Yellow Pages phone book. My mother paid him $400 to unearth my future career via aptitude testing. That was a lot of money in 1982, the equivalent of $1,150 today.

For three consecutive nights at the end of my senior year in high school, I drove to Brookdale Community College and brought my required Ticonderoga number two pencil, as instructed. Allow me to digress here; it's my ADD kicking in.

How come you have never heard of a Ticonderoga number one pencil? Or a Ticonderoga number three pencil? Or a number six one? Did they even make those versions? It was always the number two pencil requested when filling out tests where you had to color in those Scantron bubbles for the answer. Why was that? Was there Ticonderoga pencil favoritism at play here? Or pencil identity discrimination? Perhaps pencilism? Pencilphobia? Antipencilism? I wondered.

OK, I'm back now. My apologies.

After twelve hours of painstakingly answering hundreds of monotonous questions by coloring in those tiny circles to determine my eventual career, the results were sent to Marv to be evaluated. A week later, they were.

Drum roll, please . . . .

According to Marv's test, I was best suited for a career as a—wait for it—retail clothier.

Huh? . . . Nothing in music? . . . Really?

How Marv Davis came to that preposterous conclusion was anyone's guess. First off, I am color-blind. I couldn't tell you the difference between blues and purples, browns and reds and greens, and yellows and oranges. And forget about the countless other shades. Hence, there was never any color coordination or matching when dressing. You'd think that would be a prerequisite to the profession. In addition, I had zero fashion sense. All four years in high school, I wore the same bland outfit: T-shirt, Levis jeans, and black Converse high-top All-Star Chuck Taylor sneakers—years before rock stars, actors, and hipsters began wearing them as fashion statements. When I wore my Cons, they were not considered cool then, only to me and a handful of other goofballs. Boys at the time were wearing the more stylish Adidas, Puma, Pony, and new Nike sneakers. Converse were so Fifties and Sixties. *Retail clothier?* Please. Marv likely cashed my mother's $400 check, handed me some papers to fill out using my Ticonderoga number two pencil, and then randomly named any career. Why not a goat herder? Or circus impresario? Or goalie for a professional hockey team?

What about a furniture salesman? Or a shipbuilder? Or seafarer? Why not a horse trainer?

What was wrong with those career options? They were about as far-fetched as me becoming a retail clothier. Why wasn't one of those careers suggested?

GRAY SKIES: A (Moron's) Memo

    I don't recall Marv ever explaining how he arrived at his conclusion. I wanted a detailed clarification so I could understand the process. For example, when you're working out a math problem on the chalkboard in a school classroom and must arrive at the answer. The teacher scrutinizes how you reached your conclusion, and you show the sequence of steps you took to arrive there. Then, somewhere in the problem, the teacher pinpoints where you went wrong. You make the corrections and then work through the problem until you reach the correct conclusion. Not with Marv. His methodology was different. It worked like this: Give him $400, fill these ovals with a Ticonderoga number two pencil, and boom! Retail clothier. Next?

    After all that wasted vocational aptitude testing, I resigned myself to attend U.C.L.A., the University Closest to the Lincroft Area, better known to locals as Brookdale Community College. It gladly accepted D students.

While attending Brookdale, I was lost and felt like I was drowning in the middle of the ocean under a moonless, pitch-black sky. I was still dealing with both my inability to process the information I'd read and my attention deficits—two undiagnosed learning disabilities. In addition, I remained emotionally immature. I was not yet ready for college, not even community college. It would take me years before I would get my bearings. So, I did what I did best. I clowned around and treated Brookdale as a social club where I'd catch up with Geneva friends and some old Freehold friends I hadn't seen since leaving St. Mary's seven years prior. When people asked me what I was studying at Brookdale, I told them I was a double major: I was taking up time and space.

After three semesters and 18 earned credits, I dropped out. When I did, I broke my mother's heart. As her youngest child, I was her last hope to earn a college degree, which was very important to her. She viewed it as a badge of honor, proof someone was intelligent. It separated the smart people from the dummies.

My sister never went to college. She graduated from Catholic high school and immediately secured a full-time job with Bell Telephone Company. Interestingly, my mother never considered her a dummy. She considered her a career woman.

My oldest brother bailed his junior year of college, blowing his full track & field scholarship. He dropped out of my father's alma mater, Seton Hall University, to start an auto body business out of my parents' garage. Our poor neighbors! First, they were subjected to the basketball court on our side property with people bouncing balls on it during all hours of the day, then Noah's Ark in our backyard, and then the noxious paint fumes from my oldest brother's new business stinking up our block.

Brother 2 also dropped out of Seton Hall. It was a double whammy for dad, which doubled his disappointment—two of his sons dropping out of his alma mater. Brother 2 was on a partial scholarship to play football, yet during his sophomore year, Seton Hall cut the football team from the school's athletic program. When that happened, Brother 2 lost interest in college. Dismayed, he returned home, not knowing his next move. Then, one night at the dinner table, while inhaling mouthfuls of food, Brother 2 casually lifted his head and offered to no one in particular, "I just joined the Navy," before placing his head back down and continuing to fork more food.

My mother froze, the utensils dropping from her hands. "Whoa, what?" she managed to get out.

With his dark brown eyes, my father glared menacingly at my brother.

My mother asked Brother 2 to clarify: Was he *thinking* of joining the Navy, or did he actually *join* the Navy?

My eyes darted back and forth between family members. Thankfully, I was not part of the unfolding drama.

Still chewing, Brother 2 said he *joined* the Navy. My mother asked him why. While shoving a new portion of food into his mouth, my brother said he visited the recruiting offices in downtown Freehold; a one-stop shopping that housed all four military branches inside a single location. He entered the building and peeked into the first room on the right, the Marines. No recruiter was present. He turned and looked across the hall into the Air Force office. Empty. He then took a few steps down the narrow, wood-paneled hallway and peered into the Army's recruiting office. Vacant. So he turned and looked across the hall into the Navy recruiting office. He spotted a man in a bright white uniform sitting at a desk with a big grin on his clean-shaven face. The recruiter stood tall and greeted Brother 2 as if they were long-lost buddies. It was that simple. There was no comparison shopping among the armed forces beforehand. No prior meetings with vets. No discussion of pay, benefits, or training among the various military branches. Nothing. My parents sat astonished. I thought it was the one night my father had a reason to go drinking.

If you're keeping score at home, that's 0 for 4 kids at the time earning a college degree or with the promise of getting one. The good news? (Spoiler alert!) Years later, my mother was fortunate to witness two of her children graduate from college—Brother 2 and me, receiving my bachelor's degree with honors.

Looking out into the commencement audience at the Patriots Theater at the War Memorial in Trenton, I could see my mother proudly sitting upright in the second row, her blue-green eyes blazing with ecstasy. When my name was announced to receive the diploma, I proudly strutted across the stage in my cap and gown, glancing at my mother along the way. She was beaming and cheering for me. I felt like a million bucks. I'm sure that day was the day my mother officially no longer considered me a moron. I was thirty-eight.

To make money, both during my time at Brookdale and after I dropped out of Brookdale, I continued working weekends at the Englishtown Flea Market, aka the Auction, and from Monday through Friday, I began working full-time cutting lawns. That was pretty much what you did in Geneva after high school if you were a male and didn't attend college. You mowed grass or swung a hammer. The work was hard, but the pay was enticing at $6 an hour. At the time, the minimum wage was $3.35 an hour, so I earned nearly double what my non-lawn-cutting peers were making: scooping ice cream, pumping gas, flipping burgers, or working in retail. Aside from earning cash money, the perks were good. The work was outdoors; you'd get a free tan, exercise, and be able to move to various locations throughout the day. There was no monotony of sitting in the same cubicle day after day, staring at the same scenery.

    Our crew consisted of four guys. We cut between twenty-five and thirty lawns daily in the hazy, humid New Jersey summer. The business owner was a shrewd guy named Eric Niederman. He was eight years older than me, knew my oldest brother, and was smart enough never to set foot on a lawn behind a mower himself, yet he collected all the proceeds. He'd often check up on us while driving his new convertible Corvette with the top down, his beautiful brunette girlfriend Veronica seated beside him. Veronica was my age, yet traded up to date Eric because he was a handsome devil who drove a fancy car and made piles of cash from his business. In my hometown, as I saw it, if you didn't go to college, you became a drunk and/or druggie, a lawn cutter, or a carpenter. With no disrespect to drunks, junkies, lawn cutters, or carpenters, I wanted to be none of the above. But I knew I had to make money to escape Geneva to see what I would become. I realized it could take time.

One night, after cutting lawns, I went to see the movie *Trading Places* with a friend who was home on summer break from Montclair State College. After watching it, I was inspired to make as much money as possible to eventually enjoy the lavish lifestyle of the fictional Duke brothers in the film. The following day, I rose early, ready to take on the world. Instead of drinking my usual Carnation Instant breakfast mix in a glass of whole milk, I ate a bacon and egg sandwich from a local deli. I felt like a new man with that protein energy. Five hours later, I was lying unconscious in a hospital bed. Not from the breakfast food but from the fall.

As was customary in the lawn-cutting business back in the day, the pickup truck driver and one worker would sit on the bench seat inside the cab. Additional workers would stand in the back of the truck bed, sometimes on top of grass clippings, sometimes on the ridged metal bed itself, with hands on the cab's roof to provide stability and balance as the vehicle moved. Everyone in town would see you with your glorious tan, lean teenage body, Ray-Ban sunglasses, and sun-frosted hair. You looked cool. Standing in the truck's bed, the sides came up about knee-high. So if the driver made a sudden turn, there was a 50/50 chance which worker in the back would go flying out the one side. And that day, it was me. Since Danny, the driver, unexpectedly veered left at a fork in the road, traveling about thirty miles an hour, I toppled out the right side of the truck bed. As was described by an eyewitness to the accident, after flying out of the truck, I initially landed on my head before tumbling around on the hot macadam in the same spot where I held my mock religious ceremonies in the black cassock six years before. *Payback from a higher power for mocking the sanctity of a Catholic church mass ritual when I was a kid?* Perhaps.

And then I was flat and still, face down on the road's scorching pavement. The pickup truck screeched to a halt. A lady sitting on her front porch watching the event unfold in real time immediately called an ambulance. The last thing I remember was the cutting crew heading to lunch after completing thirteen lawns. The next thing I remembered was lying on a hospital gurney with unfamiliar faces staring down at me. It was three hours later when I regained consciousness. Remember my dad often told me I had rocks in my head? Maybe he was right after all. My dense head seemed to have helped me survive the fall. After all, I landed directly on my noggin after I flew out of the truck. However, hospital X-rays of my skull disproved my dad's longstanding theory. No rocks were found inside. I told my father that. He was not amused. He was more concerned with how much the hospital bill was going to cost than he was with what was inside my skull. After I spent a few days in the hospital, I was sent home to recover from my various wounds.

After three weeks of recovery, I was ready and able to return to work and eager to start making money. That was until I heard the lawn-cutting business owner, Eric, had no intention of taking me back. To add salt to my wounds, he wasn't interested in helping me pay any of my medical bills, which totaled more than two thousand dollars. The convertible Corvette-driving cheapskate never returned my calls, nor did he get back to me when I stopped by "his" home—that he lived in with his parents as a twenty-seven-year-old raking in the dough. Just saying. When I knocked on the door of "his" home, Eric's mother always answered, yet sent me on my way without letting me speak with her son. After hearing all that and feeling my frustration, my best friend Anthony strongly suggested I sue Eric. So I did. His business, anyway. That's when it was uncovered the dapper-dressed man who had enough money to drive around in his flashy new convertible Corvette, wear a Rolex watch, and don expensive clothes and jewelry did not have insurance on his work truck or his business. Talk about failing Business 101. So, my attorney had to settle on suing my car insurance company through my policy's personal injury protection coverage. We sued for the $10,000 maximum, of which my lawyer would earn a third. It took five years for me to get my share of $6,000—after the lawyer's cut and other associated expenses. But I was thrilled to have that money, as it came in handy when I purchased my first home just a few years later. As for Eric, the lawn-cutting business owner, two years after I fell from his work truck, I showed up uninvited to his new apartment for his Halloween party. When he answered the door and saw me standing there, he appeared as if he'd seen a ghost—though I was not dressed as one. I had crutches underneath both my armpits, wore a neck brace, and had my head covered in bandages doused with fake blood. I told him I was dressed for Halloween as an injured lawn cutter. He shook his head, smiled, and reluctantly invited me in.

 I sustained a lot more damage to my body than the $6,000 awarded to me as a result of the accident. My lower back has never been the same. Writing this now, some thirty-seven years later, I still feel pain in my lower back. I've tried chiropractors, yoga, inversion tables, weight loss, exercise, weight training, and funky gadgets purchased from late-night infomercials. All to no avail. Surgery was suggested—a "simple procedure" could fix the problem. That's what I was told. Not so sure about that. Keep reading, and you'll see that even "simple procedures" can sometimes have deadly consequences.

Interestingly, six months after my accident, a friend was stopped at a red light when the car behind him lightly tapped his rear bumper due to the driver momentarily taking her foot off the brake. Within a year, my buddy was awarded $18,000—his share—for a questionable injury his lawyer claimed he sustained. It took me five years to get ten grand.

It's worth mentioning a side note about my accident. Three years after I fell from the pickup truck, the #1 ranked javelin thrower in the world at the time, a six-foot-four, two-hundred-and-forty-five-pound behemoth of a man from New Jersey named Bob Roggy, also fell out the back of a pickup truck in the same manner.

What are the odds that two New Jersey javelin throwers would fall out of the back of a pickup truck in the same manner within a few years?

Tragically, unlike me, Bob Roggy died upon impact after he hit the ground. I remind myself of this fact whenever I feel luckless and the world owes me something. I was given the greatest fortune of all that scorching summer day by being granted life itself. The world owes me nothing.

CHAPTER 9

Pranks For The Memories

I returned home from community college class one overcast fall day to see a realtor's For Sale sign planted in the middle of my front lawn. *That's weird*, I thought—excellent work by my prankster friend, Michael Michaels. Over the years, we'd often one-up each other with such antics.

When I was eleven, pretending to be Michael's mother, I called a tow truck company to remove Michael's mother's car from her driveway. While I was giggling my ass off watching the events unfold from my backyard, Michael's mom was screaming at the tow truck driver to release the hooked-up car in her driveway, claiming it must be a mistake, that she hadn't called to have it towed. A few weeks later, Michael retaliated by pretending to be my mother, calling a landscaping supplier, and ordering a multi-cubic yard delivery of topsoil from a local nursery to be dumped smack in the middle of my driveway. Thankfully, my mom was home to run outside and halt the action just as the driver was about to release the dump, demanding to know who authorized the delivery. As pranks, we'd call for cabs, pizza, and Chinese food to be delivered to each other's homes. Those practical jokes went back and forth but eventually died off. I wondered why the game suddenly resurfaced after being dormant for years.

I yanked the for sale sign out from the ground, walked it over to Michael's home a house away, and plunged it into his front yard. Just after I did, Michael's watchful mother poked her head out her front door and asked me what in God's name I was doing. I told her the joke her son played on me by putting the sign on my lawn. Mrs. Michaels said Michael wasn't home; he was in Upstate New York with his father. She advised me to take the sign back home and talk to my parents. So I did.

In one of the rare moments my parents were not quarreling, they sat me down at the dining room table and broke the news as a unified front with solemn expressions. We were moving. After a moment of stunned disbelief, a sense of complete helplessness washed over me. My hopes of living in that house for at least a few more years to figure out a life course had been dashed. I was nineteen, with the maturity level of a thirteen-year-old boy. I had much maturing to do. And by the presence of the For Sale sign, it appeared I had to start that maturation process rather quickly.

My parents purchased the home in 1962 for $19,000. Twenty-one years later, they were listing it for $86,000. That was the good news. The bad news was that my parents were in debt up to their eyeballs then. My father had been consistently unemployed for years and only worked sporadically before that. That didn't help their financial situation. As a result, my parents wouldn't have much left over after they sold their home and squared up with their creditors—including a dear friend of my mother who lived up the block. One week after my house was officially listed on the market, it sold. The new owners were scheduled to take possession thirty short days later. Life-altering events seemed to be happening at warp speed, and I began fretting over the situation. Unbeknownst to me, my mother rented me a room in a home down the block and around the corner. The house was owned by a twenty-five-year-old yuppie named Kevin Horvath. Kevin had recently purchased the 4-bedroom house similar to the one I lived in, occupied one bedroom, and rented out the three other bedrooms for $400 a month each. The young man just moved into the neighborhood, so it was not like our family knew the guy to be able to vet him. He could have been an ax murderer, which probably would have been OK with my dad. If he had the money, my dad might have even bought Kevin a new ax. Somehow, my mom came across Kevin and negotiated the deal, letting him know I was a good boy, no trouble, and a worthy candidate to become a $400-a-month tenant in his house.

It worked. The power of a concerned mom on display.

One interesting fact about my future home: it was located directly across the street from Mandy Evans's house, my girlfriend during the summer between seventh and eighth grade. If you'd told the thirteen-year-old me, while I was hanging out with Mandy during that glorious and carefree summer of 1977, that six years later, I would be living in the house across the street with a bunch of strangers because my parents moved to Virginia, I never would have believed you. Not in a hundred years. There would never be a need to move. In my town, families moved because dads got transferred to another state due to their jobs. My dad didn't have a job. He was unemployed. Also, our family was a staple in the community for two decades.

During earlier sober years, my father coached hundreds of kids in youth basketball. He was once a respected and enduring fixture in our community and recognized as our town's best pool player. Everybody knew my mother, and some appreciated her acerbic wit and bluntness. My oldest brother was a local legend with his track accolades, his customized candy apple red VW Bug, and his handsome looks, including a killer mustache. And Brother 2 was a superior all-around athlete who dated half the girls in the town, eagerly waiting to date the other half when he returned home on leave from the Navy. I was also part of the community, making a name for myself as a wacky yet sociable kid and a good athlete who played the guitar and had a vast network of friends. My parents would never move from Geneva. Why would they? And Virginia? *Why there?*

Fast-forward six years, and there I was in that exact predicament: indescribably unhappy with how my life was changing and with nothing I could do to stop it.

I later came to find out the move was necessary for my father to become sober and find work and for my parents to hit the reset button on their lives. They were both in their mid-fifties, and such a move was difficult to do with kids, grandkids, friends, and a life, memories, and community they'd be leaving behind. As crucial as that home was to me, it was infinitely more important to my mother. She always claimed that Cape Cod house was her favorite out of all the many homes she ever lived in while married to my father. It broke her heart to leave it, which broke my heart.

Only a few days after I'd gotten the unwanted news that our home was for sale, my dad and I came to blows. Due to the pending move, every household resident was on edge, and the tension was palpable. My father and I were two separate volcanoes with pressure building, preparing to explode. And then they did.

    One day, I was running late for my macroeconomics class at community college and heading out the door when my mother asked me to bring in the metal garbage cans from the curb. I promised I would when I returned home. Standing in the kitchen near my mother, my father ordered me to return. Like most teens, I rolled my eyes and exhaled out loud before heading into the kitchen. My dad's jaw was clenched, and his eyes narrowed. Without saying a word, my father threw a right cross that landed square on my jaw. Dazed, I staggered backward from the unexpected blow. Once the cobwebs cleared, I remember thinking *No way!* My boiling point reached, I snapped under the pressure and did something I had never done. I lunged at my father and grabbed him in a bear hug, lifted his body six inches off the ground, and slammed him to the floor. My father landed in the corner of the kitchen with me on top of him, straddling his torso in the mounted position, rendering him immobile. Adrenaline surging through my body and filled with rage, I tightened my left hand around his neck and held my right fist above his head, threatening a punch. A look of panic washed across his face. His eyes were bulging, and he was squirming to get me off him. But he could not move me. The tables were turned. I was the one wielding power over him. Shocked at what she was witnessing, my mother screamed at me in a strange voice I never heard before to get off him, that he was my father. As I sat atop my father's torso, I kept telling him he was an alcoholic loser, taunting him to hit me, and asking him how it felt to be the one getting bullied. I had always been intimidated by my father, but I saw fear in his eyes. It was the first time in my life that I did. It made me even more empowered. Still on top of him and rendering him motionless, I roared, releasing years of frustration, hurt, and pain.

By this time, my mother was hysterical, hitting me with a dishrag with her right hand while trying to pull me off him with her left. After a minute of being on top of my father, I slowly got to my feet, panting from the adrenaline dump and energy expended to keep him pinned down. My father slowly rose, never taking his eyes off me. He was hyperventilating, and beads of sweat covered his face. For a moment, I thought he might be having a heart attack. He ran his hands through his disheveled, full head of thick salt-and-pepper hair and then shuffled out of the small kitchen with his head down, defeated. In front of his wife. By his youngest son. My mother began shouting at me that I had to leave the house immediately or she was going to call the police and have me arrested. Have *me* arrested.

Feeling completely betrayed because my mother sided with my father, who threw the first punch, I rushed to my bedroom, grabbed my car keys and guitar, and stormed out of the house. I sped away and slept in my Beetle in another part of town that night. The following afternoon, I returned home only to be welcomed by a black Hefty garbage bag sitting on my front porch. A note was Scotch-taped to it in my mother's handwriting, saying I was no longer welcome in the house. The garbage bag contained some of my clothes and toiletries. I plucked it from the porch, tossed it into my VW, and sat in my car, trying to figure out where to go. Anthony was in college on the other side of the state, Bobby was out of state at Salem College in West Virginia, and Mehmet was halfway around the world in Turkey, visiting his family for a couple of months. So, I drove to my new friend Seth Miller's home to decompress and process matters. Seth was not there, but his mother was. I let her know what happened and that I was essentially kicked out of my home for defending myself after being sucker-punched by my father. Sensing my unease, Mrs. Miller allowed me to stay at her home for the next three weeks, allowing me access to her oldest son's bedroom since he was away at law school in California. During my time at Seth's home, his mom and my mom contacted each other daily to discuss my status since I wouldn't take my mother's frequent calls. It was a mess.

I experienced a mixture of feelings, from shame and remorse to pride and anger at what I had done to my father. But I'd do it all again if he ever laid another hand on me. After three weeks, I was given the green light to return home. When I did, I had the upper hand. I was no longer afraid of my father. Seeing what I was capable of, he was afraid of me.

My life was in utter turmoil. Being faced with having to move was impossible for my brain to process. My father and I couldn't stand each other, making for a challenging living situation. And my house was about to have new owners occupying it in just a few weeks. I was struggling with my studies at college and didn't know where my life was heading. I had to sort things out and needed emotional support and guidance to help get me through this tough time. I was still dating Diane, who was a senior in high school. I turned to her for emotional support. What can I say? She was my girlfriend, and I was a glutton for punishment. Remember: the subtitle of this book is a *moron's* memoir—not a *genius's* memoir.

Like Charlie Brown foolishly expecting Lucy to hold the football while he tries to kick it, Lucy does what Lucy does; she yanks the ball away just as Charlie attempts to make contact with it. He falls flat on his back, and Lucy crows at poor old Charlie Brown. I didn't know where else to go to get that emotional support. My friends were great, but they were also dimwitted teenage boys. Not the greatest givers of emotional support. Besides, they were all busy studying and partying on college campuses scattered about the Northeast. As far as my three siblings, they were all busy living their lives without me in it. Brother 2 was in the Navy, halfway around the world, in the Mediterranean Sea off the coast of Haifa, Israel. Doing what, I have no idea. Brother 1 was busy as a newlywed husband, new father, and business owner living and working in other towns. My sister was busy living and working in South Jersey, raising her two daughters in her second marriage. I rarely saw or spoke to them—the usual. That's why I sought Diane to help me figure things out. As usual, things backfired.

Diane agreed to meet at my home at 8 pm to discuss my pending life-changing situation. The plans were set, and I was looking forward to seeing her to discuss the matter and our future. My parents were going out with friends that night, which would provide us alone time to talk . . . and hopefully more. Eight o'clock came and went without Diane showing up or calling. Feeling unsettled, I phoned her home at 8:15 p.m. and got her on the line. Diane reported she was sick, had a fever, and was going to stay home and sleep. She coughed a few times on the phone for good measure, apologized, and asked if we could reschedule. *Of course*, I told her, wishing her well and letting her know I hoped she felt better, I'd call her tomorrow, and that I loved her.

About an hour later, while playing my guitar in my bedroom, doubts began to creep into my head, and my Spidey senses kicked in. Hmm. *Was she really sick?* To find out, I drove to her house three miles away. Diane's car was parked in the driveway, which was a good sign she was telling the truth. I knocked on her front door. A moment later, her elderly mother appeared, a thick bob of hair atop her smallish head and a cigarette dangling between two bony fingers. In a gravelly voice cultivated after years of smoking cigarettes, she let me know Diane was not home. Friends had picked her up to go to a party to meet up with some boys.

Standing on the front porch, I felt like a mule kicked me in the gut. Misled. Again.

Diane's mother smirked, knowing full well what she was doing by relinquishing the goods on her daughter's departure. She spurted a jet of cigarette smoke before taking another puff from her cancer stick, the chasms in her face moving as she did. Then she went on a machine-gun monologue, yapping about how disrespectful Diane has been to her, citing the most recent examples in a lengthy and blistering critique. I thanked her in mid-sentence, then split. As I hurried to my VW Bug parked on the street, Diane's mother was still complaining about her daughter. Dejected and irritated, I returned home and made calls to inquire about Diane's whereabouts. A half-hour later, I found out where she was. And I decided to pay that home a surprise visit.

When I entered the split-level house, I barely recognized most of the two dozen or so partygoers. It was a mix of older burnouts in their early twenties and a handful of dirtbag townies I barely knew. People I was warned to stay away from. It seemed everyone stopped what they were doing and turned to look at me. It was apparent my entrance was a surprise, and I felt jarringly out of place. But I didn't care. I was on a mission. The moment reminded me of those EF Hutton commercials people of a certain age are sure to remember, where everyone stopped what they were doing to hear what EF Hutton had to say. Joan Jett's "Bad Reputation" was blaring from the stereo in the living room. Nodding to people I walked past, I spotted a few of Diane's friends huddled together in the kitchen by the tapped keg of beer, red plastic Solo cups clutched in their hands. Older guys I didn't know were cozying up to them. When Diane's friends spotted me, their eyes widened. One friend cautiously approached me and questioned what I was doing there. She told me Diane wasn't there and asked me to leave, but I wasn't buying it, and I wasn't leaving. I brushed past her and walked from room to room until I could locate my girlfriend. After no luck searching the first floor, I plodded upstairs and opened the door to the first bedroom on the left. Bingo! Diane was buck naked in bed, lying on her back with some derelict who dropped out of school a year before on top of her, thrusting away. I was shocked, she was shocked, and the guy was shocked. We were all shocked. I screamed she was my girlfriend, and with all my might, I grabbed the naked dude by the arm and yanked him out of bed. At his most vulnerable, he scrambled to clutch a bed sheet and covered himself with it before scampering out of the room. Even when I caught my girlfriend having sex with someone else and had incontrovertible evidence—my own eyes—Diane claimed it was a misunderstanding.

How could his penis in your vagina be a misunderstanding? I shouted.

Staring into Diane's bloodshot eyes, I could see she was under the influence of something. Diane and her friends often took diet pills—amphetamines—and hallucinogenic mushrooms, aka magic mushrooms, when drinking alcohol. This supposedly was to achieve a more significant high. I wouldn't know. I wasn't into that shit. God knows what Diane was on. The girl looked completely wasted.

I was crushed, angry, and confused. *How could you do this to me?* I kept asking her over and over. Having had enough of my interrogation, Diane jumped out of bed and spit in my face. I was stunned and couldn't believe it. I didn't know how to react. I just stood there, a nasty mix of her ejected phlegm and saliva clinging to my forehead and cheek before I wiped off the gobs with my coat sleeve. I should have been spitting in her face for spinning lies and weaving a tapestry of deceit over the last two years. Just then, a few people barged into the room—including the girl who lived there—and ordered me to leave the house immediately. I raised my hands to show no resistance as they surrounded me and escorted me down the stairs and out of the home. My head was spinning, and I felt completely alone. I left the party a heartbroken mess, vowing never to see Diane again or trust another girl again.

Thirty days after my home sold, a giant 18-wheel Mayflower moving truck was parked in my driveway. Burly, unkempt movers, one black and one white, emptied the contents from my soon-to-be former home and packed them into the truck. I stood on my soon-to-be former front porch in silence, watching the scene play out, my friends Mehmet and Anthony at my side, their hands upon each of my shoulders, doing their best to comfort me. I succumbed to an avalanche of emotions from sadness to fear to anxiety to anger to disappointment to loneliness. My dad and I still weren't speaking, so I bid goodbye to my mother only, tears in her eyes, tears in mine as we embraced. My mother wanted me to live with them in Virginia, but there was no way that would ever happen. My dad and I despised each other.

Watching the moving truck slowly roll away, my parents following in their 1980 Pontiac Lemans, I waved at my mom in the front passenger seat. As the car crawled behind the moving truck, my mother craned her neck to keep me in sight until I receded from view. My parents' car slowly disappeared into the distance as tears trickled down my cheeks. That sight is forever embedded in my memory. If I live to be a hundred, I'll never forget it.

The new homeowners began moving their belongings inside, courtesy of their movers. It was a surreal experience—like I was watching a movie, and everything was happening to someone else. But it wasn't. It was happening to me. I was now standing on *their* front porch. They were nice people who let me overstay my time on their property, but the husband-and-wife duo eventually gave me a look like it was time to go.

Anthony and Mehmet escorted me down the steps, off the property, and onto the street, where the tears continued to slide down my face. I hugged and thanked my buddies, wiped my eyes, climbed into my VW Bug, started her up to the usual noisy coughs and sputters, and drove away. I met up with Mehmet later that night, and we headed down to the shore to escape the earlier traumatic events of the day. Half past midnight, I dropped Mehmet off safely at his home. Due to my compromised state of mind and alcohol consumption, I completely forgot about my new living arrangements and mistakenly pulled into the driveway of my former home. I parked in my usual spot off to the side and walked up the few porch steps as I'd done countless times during my nineteen years there. Once on the front porch, I began fumbling with my house keys trying to unlock the door, but for some reason could not. None of my keys seemed to work. The scenario seemed eerily familiar. Only now, it was me outside the front door, drunk and swaying, instead of my father. After a minute, the inside lights turned on.

Good, I thought, *my mom is going to let me in*. The front door slowly opened just far enough to allow the chain to be latched inside. But it was not my mom standing beyond the door. The new Filipina owner let me know she would call the police if I did not leave the property immediately. Trying to process what was happening, I apologized, turned around, and tromped down the porch steps slump-shouldered with my head in my hands. It took me a moment to regain my bearings. Then I realized the situation. I climbed back into my Bug, drove to my new home down the block and around the corner, and parked on the street. Rather than enter my new house and crash in my private bedroom, I felt a gravitational pull back to my former home. So, I stumbled back to it using the sidewalk and quietly crawled into the tall bushes underneath my former first-floor bedroom window, the one facing the basketball court. And the memories. That was a safe hiding place where I'd sometimes go to escape life when things got out of control and to reflect on whatever lousy situation I was in. I sat on the frigid ground, buried my face in my hands, and wept. I eventually nodded off to sleep and awoke a few hours later while it was still dark. Sobered up, I strolled to my new house down the block, entered, and felt like I was in a strange place where I did not belong.

While I was doing my best as a teenager living alone for the first time, I struggled. Mightily at times.

I soon dropped out of college and began working full-time as a fuel transport engineer—aka pumping gas—at the Power Test on Route 9, a few miles from my new residence. My newest housemates were five and seven years older, had zero in common with me, and were considerably more mature. They were all nice guys, college-educated and working professionals, and all that. But they were not my friends. As such, I did my best to spend as little time as possible in that house. My bills began to mount in no time, and I could not earn enough to pay them all, no matter how many double shifts I worked pumping gas. I was in a funk and sometimes had no money to buy food. I was surviving on three-for-a-dollar packs of ramen noodles. I occasionally resorted to looting my housemates' bread or peanut butter while they slept, quietly eating in my tiny rented room so as not to awaken them. When eating their food was not an option, I'd walk over to the Grand Union supermarket outside my development in the wee hours of the morning and scope out the scene. Between 3 a.m. and 3:30 a.m., milk and bread trucks made their deliveries. I'd sit watching from a wooded area fifteen yards away, waiting for the right moment to strike. When the drivers would walk away from their trucks to smoke a cigarette or a joint or relieve themselves on the side of the building, I'd sneak up to the back of the trucks and snatch a gallon of milk and a loaf of whatever bread I could grab, then dash back into the woods. Undetected, like a ninja thief. When the coast was clear, I'd walk those stolen goods a half-mile back to my home, crossing the four-lane Route Nine.

Repeat as necessary. Desperate times called for desperate measures. Lord knows I was desperate.

My mom called my new house every few days to ask how I was doing. Using the one house phone located on the kitchen wall, I assured her I was fine (I wasn't), I was eating (I was barely), and I was still attending college (I'd dropped out). I refrained from telling her the truth. The woman was dealing with her own pain and adjusting to a new life down in Virginia.

During my five months in that rented room, I often showed up like an alley cat behind the Kismet Diner, a few miles up Route Nine north. My friend Mehmet's Turkish family owned it. Too embarrassed to say I was ravenously hungry, I'd mill about by the diner's back door near the dumpsters, pacing around until someone spotted me, eddies of wind whirling dirt and paper garbage into spirals as I waited. Due to the extreme heat in the kitchen, the back door was always open, no matter the season. So it would only be a few minutes before one of Mehmet's family members would see me through the screen door. Taking pity on me, Mehmet's brother, father, sister, or mother would invite me in and sit me down at a booth, hand me a menu, and tell me to order anything I wanted. I'd sheepishly let them know I had no money. Mehmet's family members always told me I never needed it there. I was generously offered steaks, chops, fish—anything on the menu. But I ordered the same meal every time: a bowl of white rice with tomato sauce on top and a glass of chocolate milk. When I placed my order, Mehmet's family member would always shake their head, persuading me to eat a better meal—whatever I wanted. Pork chops? Filet mignon? Chilean sea bass? Veal? Chicken parmesan? Spaghetti and meatballs? Anything. Without cost to me.

But I always wanted a big bowl of white rice with tomato sauce and chocolate milk. And that's what they always gave me. Once delivered, I'd stare at it wide-eyed, taking it all in before devouring it. Afterward, I'd hold my stomach with a big, satisfied grin. And then, I would thank them for their kindness and generosity.

D

The thing about my former hometown is that most guys lived at home with their parents into their late twenties. Some were even in their thirties. The latter group often used the old switcheroo to deflect criticism, telling people their parents lived *with them*. I used the acronym ILAH (I Live At Home) to describe those dependent moochers. Girls in my hometown swooned over that kind of guy. These grown men paid no rent and typically drove a new Corvette, BMW, Trans Am, or Camaro IROC. They wore flashy clothes and jewelry, had money to burn, and possessed confidence in spades. When I'd point out to girls that a particular guy was twenty-eight or thirty years old and was still living at home with his parents—which was the reason he could afford to drive an expensive IROC, Beamer, Trans Am, or Corvette—the girls would either tell me I was jealous (I was) or they didn't care (They didn't). I detested ILAHs. Hated them. They always had girls on their arms, and I didn't. They were the same guys who would gladly accept a beer from you at a bar but would never buy you one in return. Though they lived rent-free with their parents and had a surplus of cash, they were cheapskates. Not my kind of guys.

    With my closest friends, Anthony, Dave, Joel, and Joe, away at college and Mehmet working at his family's diner full time, I began spending more time with my newest friend, Seth Miller. An adrift pothead, he wasn't the best influence for me, but as a townie, he was present, like me. I felt bad for the kid. His dad had passed away a couple of years before, and his mother had just sold her home and fled to Southern California while he stayed put in Geneva. Aside from Seth, I also began hanging out with various second and third-tier level friends. They were typical blue-collar Geneva guys working in landscaping or construction, with a few looking for work. At least two were on track to make future appearances in rehab for substance abuse. As I said, they were not the best people for me to be associating with, but they were guys who were all available.

    Most would end up marrying a hometown girl, have a few kids they'd raise in that same town they'd never leave, and ones who would constantly reminisce about their high school days with their buddies. But that wasn't what I wanted.

    Hanging with my new friends, sometimes I would be the life of the party, playing my guitar and telling funny stories to entertain. I'd often have people in stitches. But the reality was that at the end of the night, they all returned to their parents' comfy homes—where they'd lived rent-free—while Seth slept in his car, and I returned to a $400-a-month rented room in a house full of strangers. My home and Seth's home were gone, and our parents were gone as well—his dad, forever. My parents lived 200 miles away in Northern Virginia, and Seth's mom lived 2,800 miles away in Southern California. At the end of the night, I'd get a shoulder clap, man-hug, or handshake and some words about how great it was to see me and how crazy or funny a particular story of mine was, but no one invited me to their homes for a home-cooked meal the next night. And no one ever invited Seth to their homes so he could sleep in a warm bed rather than a cold car. Seth and I were often the life of the parties yet shunned when they ended. We felt abandoned. It was a sobering realization that we were both on our own.

As bad as my situation was, I knew Seth's was worse. As such, I wanted to help him, perhaps playing the role of a big brother who cares. Seth's mother helped me by allowing me to live in her home after my parents tossed me out. So, it was the least I could do for her son, my latest friend.

My landlord, Kevin—who owned and lived in the home he rented to others—strictly forbade non-residents from entering his house under any circumstances. He made that crystal clear on day one. If anyone violated the rule, we'd be evicted. It would not matter what the circumstances were. His tenants had to acknowledge this with a signature on the rental agreement. Kevin said that even if supermodels Christie Brinkley or Cindy Crawford wanted to enter his home with one of his tenants, they would be kicked out, along with us, and our rental agreement would be terminated.

Despite the consequences of violating that rule, I snuck Seth into Kevin's house a few nights a week in the wee hours of the morning while everyone was asleep to allow him to crash on my bedroom floor. It was a better option than Seth sleeping in the backseat of his car parked behind the mini-mart, especially during New Jersey's frigid fall nights. After a good night's sleep on my carpeted floor, Seth would shower and then slip out the back door after my housemates went to work. It was better than him washing and brushing his teeth at the sink in the local Shell gas station's disgusting bathroom. Occasionally, a housemate would question if I had brought someone into the house late at night. I'd lie and deny it. Landlord Kevin reminded me of the consequences if I did. The sleep-shower routine with Seth went smoothly for a few weeks before it all blew up one day.

First, you must know that although Seth was an intelligent and creative eighteen-year-old, he was not playing with a full deck. Far from it. Though he had a girlfriend and was not gay, one of his favorite pastimes was singing original jingles. He wrote one about our mutual friend who was gay, focusing specifically on that particular friend's buttocks. Not sure why. He was a crazy kid with a weird fixation that generated different reactions from people: laughter due to his creative rhymes, questions of his sexuality, and shakes of the head due to the immaturity of the content—something expected of a silly boy half his age. Seth claimed he sang his songs the best in the shower. It was a habit he'd been doing for years. The scene was set.

After sleeping on my tiny rented bedroom's floor, Seth was in the shower the next morning while my landlord and fellow housemates were all at work. As usual, while enjoying the hot water, Seth began belting out his songs about his friend's ass and how his friend is gay, and so on. By the way, the friend's name was Mike—the same as my name. Keep this in mind as you continue reading.

Having just showered minutes before, I was butt naked in my bedroom, drying myself off with a towel and preparing to dress, when I heard the front door slam. A voice called out, "Who's in here?"

I froze. It was my landlord, Kevin. And he was not happy.

Panicked, I ducked into my bedroom's tiny closet, quietly closed the door, and squatted in a fetal position. I placed clothes over my head to increase my chances of not being seen. I simultaneously heard two things: footsteps plodding up the stairs and Seth singing at the top of his lungs, "Mike's ass, Mike's ass, it's as fine as Waterford Crystal glass..."

Pop quiz: What do you think landlord Kevin assumed when he heard an unknown man singing a song about a guy named Mike and his fine ass? (You're right!) Remember: this was in early 1984. Being gay was not widely accepted, let alone celebrated, back then like it is today.

Landlord Kevin barged into the bathroom, ripped open the shower curtain—I can still remember the sound the metal rings made against the metal rod—and thundered, "WHO THE HELL ARE YOU? GET OUTTA MY HOUSE RIGHT NOW BEFORE I CALL THE POLICE!" I heard a shriek, then cackling and fast footsteps scampering down the hall and the stairs. Then I listened to the front door slam again. The next thing I knew, I heard slow footsteps coming my way.

"Mike, are you in here?" Kevin barked as he opened the bedroom door and entered my room. I remained silent and unmoving in my closet, wishing Kevin would disappear. The closet door opened a crack, a sliver of light shining in. I stared at the opening, hoping and praying it would not widen. A few moments went by, and I thought Kevin left the room. Just when I was making my escape plan from the house, the closet door fully opened. Though clothes sat atop my head and shoulders, my eyes were visible, and they met Kevin's eyes. Furious, Kevin questioned me if I was having sex with the "singing wacko" he just kicked out of the house. After standing up with a towel around my waist, I told Kevin that Seth was my friend who had recently lost his dad, was homeless and was living in his car. I provided him with a warm place to sleep at night and shower in the morning. As I began to pack my belongings and leave his house for good, Kevin let me slide, to my shock and surprise. However, he did say that the next time any friend of mine ever set foot in his house under any circumstances, I'd be gone that same day.

    I wasn't sure Kevin bought my story, though it was true. He both heard and observed compelling evidence to the contrary: a naked and peculiar young man in his shower singing about a guy named Mike—*my name*—and his fine ass.

I enjoyed my hometown of Geneva, New Jersey. The above story aside, I had some special memories with my friends, sports, the woods, girlfriends pre-Diane, and the community. I was blessed to have grown up in that small town during a time when neighbors made real connections—not just hollow Facebook ones. We left our windows open and our doors unlocked at night. Despite my appreciation for that hometown, for my sanity, I knew it was time to leave. The above story was only one of the impetuses that convinced me I needed a change of scenery and a place to heal from all the bad memories of my hometown. I knew just where to go.

CHAPTER 10
Lost and Found

One night, I was at a local Geneva party with fellow recent high school graduates who were not attending college, aka 'townies.' My new shower-singing friend Seth was there, surrounded by guys who looked up to him due to his history of lunacy. Halfway through the night, Seth announced that he was moving to California in two weeks. His mother had just bought a condo in the San Fernando Valley, yet she would remain in New Jersey for the summer to tie up some legal and life matters. This meant that Seth would have the entire condo all to himself for three months. He invited anyone interested to live with him during that time. He made his pitch: sunny California, no rent, hot California girls, LA and Hollywood, and the many notable seaside towns and expansive beaches.

Throughout the evening, several townies convincingly claimed they'd move out west with Seth. But I knew none of them would move out of their parent's homes, let alone out of

Geneva and across the country to California. They were townies for life. They weren't moving anywhere. But I had no heart to burst their bubbles by reminding them of that reality. At the night's end, I called Seth aside and asked him how many guys he thought would take him up on his offer. He smiled, inhaled his Marlboro red cigarette, and murmured probably just me. Well, he was right.

Perhaps driven by a psychological imperative to enter a new era or a new state with a clean slate, I decided to throw caution to the wind and go. I told Seth such and that my word was good. He was thrilled to hear the news.

I gave two weeks' notice at my full-time job pumping gas at the Power Test. I provided two weeks' notice to my landlord and left my rented room in a house a couple of blocks from where I was born and raised. I sold my VW Bug and some possessions—including my high school varsity jacket—and purchased a one-way airline ticket from Newark to Los Angeles at the local travel agency. And I left my friends behind in wet, cold, and slushy New Jersey and happily boarded the plane.

I remember being on that nonstop flight from Newark to LA, struggling to breathe due to the many smokers on the plane puffing away, clouds of toxins hovering in the air above me. As someone with asthma, the six-hour flight seemed like sixty. I couldn't wait to deplane. I was ecstatic when the captain finally announced we'd be landing shortly. I lifted the shade on the small window and could not believe what I saw below. Sunny blue skies, tall palm trees, and a majestic mountain range in the backdrop. The scene was spectacular.

Once I landed at LAX, I hitch-hiked to Calabasas in the San Fernando Valley to the address Seth provided me. I was practically giddy.

Now that I was officially in Los Angeles, I had secretly hoped to be discovered by a Hollywood agent, casting director, or producer and become famous. Maybe I would be the next big thing so I could make my fortune in music or film. Dreaming is free, right?

I lived with Seth in sunny Southern California for ten fun-filled weeks. During my second month there, it dawned on me that Hollywood was not looking to discover and make famous dim-witted young men from New Jersey with questionable talent, limited work experience, and no life direction. Shocker, I know.

While I had a fantastic time exploring that part of the country, I did nothing productive—no job, no school. I just enjoyed the perfect weather, the sights, and the experience, getting my head and thoughts in order and living off the $1,000 in cash I brought.

On my first day in the Golden State, I purchased a Fender acoustic guitar for $200, which left me $800 for the remainder of my stay. By then, I had acquired the skill of stretching a dollar. It helped that cheese sandwiches were cheap, and I didn't eat much beyond that. Seth and I enjoyed the nightlife and driving his motorcycle around the winding canyon roads and up and down the spectacular Pacific Coast Highway scenery. While out and about, we met several characters and made some interesting memories living together in his mother's condo. It was a wild adventure, for sure. And it was precisely what I needed to heal the psychological wounds of being uprooted from my childhood home, dealing with the breakup of my double-crossing girlfriend, and escaping an undesirable living situation back east. When my money ran out, I needed to split. So I did.

After ten weeks of living in California in the summer of 1984, I caught a ride back east with Seth's brother, Ethan. Ethan had just finished his semester at Pepperdine University Law School in Malibu and was itching to return to Jersey to enjoy his summer with his hometown friends. Ethan crammed volumes of his law books, my acoustic guitar, and our respective duffel bags in his 1982 Datsun 200SX, and together we drove 3,000 miles back east.

Although traversing the country from California to New Jersey was an epic road trip due to the incredible beauty of the changing landscape, Ethan's car was slightly larger than a grocery shopping cart. It did not make for a comfortable ride for either of us. For 3,000 miles, I felt like I was a fetus, contorting my six-foot-two-inch frame into the cramped interior, with no room to move my appendages. We drove through the Mojave Desert and made our first overnight stop in Scottsdale, Arizona. From there, we took turns driving straight through to St. Louis, Missouri, where we caught a Mets vs. Cardinals baseball game at Busch Stadium before crashing at a cheap motel room along the Mississippi River. The next day, we made our way to Kentucky, where we stayed overnight at Ethan's law school buddy's home. He had a gorgeous sister who Ethan told me not to even think about; she was way out of my league and only dates uber-rich older men. Then we headed to Baltimore to sleep the night at some fleabag hotel. Throughout the night, I heard what I thought were firecrackers, believing it to be an early Fourth of July celebration. I later learned they were gunshots.

On our final leg of the trip, Ethan and I drove up 95 North to New Jersey. After an exhaustive forty hours of driving, I could not wait to return home. But my unbridled joy was short-lived.

Somehow, I escaped the realization that I had no home. Upon leaving the New Jersey Turnpike at exit 8, transferring onto Route 33 East, and heading to my former hometown of Geneva, Ethan stumped me with a simple question: "Where do you want me to drop you off?"

I stared at him with an open mouth, not knowing how to respond. A lonely feeling washed over me like a tidal wave, and panic began to set in. *Wait—am I . . . homeless?* I mused.

That realization caused guilt, fear, and bewilderment to collide within me: guilt for not taking my mother's offer to live with her in Virginia, fear of where I was to go, and bewilderment as to why I hadn't planned better before I climbed into Ethan's clown car back in Malibu to come 'home.'

I hadn't seen or spoken to my sister in two years, wasn't sure where she lived, and didn't even know her phone number. Brother 2 was living on a Navy ship somewhere on the waters off the coast of North Africa, likely swabbing decks and busy searching for one of the few female sailors on the ship to hook up with during his free time. The only sibling left was my oldest brother, Brother 1. So I told Ethan to drop me off at Brother 1's house in Freehold. Fifteen minutes later, Ethan pulled into my oldest brother's driveway.

Brother 1 was sitting on his ride-on mower cutting his side lawn when we rolled up. Ethan bid me farewell. I exited his car and thanked him. He waved to Brother 1 and quickly sped to his next destination. There I was, standing and holding my guitar and duffel bag, a cloud of dirt kicked up from the unpaved driveway swirling around me.

Awk-ward!

Brother 1 turned off the engine, hopped down from his mower, and slowly shuffled over to me. His only acknowledgment as he neared was a slight nod of the head.

"Sup?" he asked, stone-faced.

I nodded and cleared my throat. "Hey," I responded.

His eyes moved to the duffel bag I held in my left hand. He grinned slightly and quizzically lifted one eyebrow.

"So, uh, that mean you need a place to stay?"

I scratched at the back of my neck and cleared my throat again. "Uh, yeah. I think so," I sheepishly replied, my eyes cast downward to the tattered black Converse hi-top sneakers on my long, skinny feet. "Not sure for how long."

Thankfully, Brother 1 and his wife were kind enough to open their home to me, especially when they already had a full house with two young daughters—my adorable nieces—three years and six months old at the time.

I needed privacy and did not want to disturb them, and since I was allergic to cats, I asked if I could stay in their 140-year-old barn fifty feet from their house. Brother 1 said if I could clean out a space, I could sleep in it. So I did, on the first floor. The space was roughly six feet by nine feet and covered in old barn dust. He offered to run a power cord out to the structure so I could have electricity. And that's where I stayed the summer of 1984. I still suffered from asthma, so living in a barely habitable, musty old barn that had no ventilation and was jam-packed with decades-old dusty junk was probably not the best thing for my respiratory system. But it was a free-living arrangement and the only home I had. I was thankful. Behind the barn was my brother-in-the-Navy's blue 1972 VW Beetle with the key in the ignition. The car started and ran, which was a remarkable stroke of good fortune. I had wheels to get around.

Back on my old stomping grounds, I connected with some high school friends at home on summer break from college. We enjoyed good times, most especially down at the Jersey Shore. It was great to see them, yet doing so was a stark reminder that they were moving in a positive direction, and I was not. My loneliness caught up with me one night, and against my better judgment, I connected with my former girlfriend, Diane Macaluso. I know, I know. What was I thinking? She was home on break from her secretarial school in North Jersey, and I was lonely. One plus one equals two. We saw each other twice during that summer. The interesting thing was that I felt nothing for her. Zero. Zilch. *Nada*. Whatever chemistry I previously had for the girl completely evaporated. Gone. The spell she held on me was finally broken, which was a relief. I wondered, though, would Diane ever change? Would a cheater ever be faithful? Were there twelve-step rehab programs for the compulsive unfaithful? If so, could a coldhearted girl, in time, become a warmhearted woman? Would future men in Diane's life be mistreated and humiliated the way she emotionally abused and humiliated me? Assuming she's married now, is her husband questioning her fidelity? Is he feeling the mistrust and anxiety I felt with her as a teenager? Did Diane eventually grow out of her cheating ways and become faithful? Or is she doing now what she did forty years ago and then talking her way out of it, blinking those big brown doe eyes at the person whose heart she's crushing? Thankfully, I'd never know. The summer of 1984 was the last time I saw or spoke to her.

While living in Brother 1's mid-19th century barn, between episodes of dawdling, I sanded and prepped cars at Brother 1's body shop to earn money. In addition, I painted homes for two different house painters in my former hometown, earning decent money in both jobs. My work allowed me to get by and have a few extra bucks for fun. While my brother and sister-in-law fed me and made me feel at home, I always felt like I was intruding. Probably because I was. When on my brother's property, I played with my precious nieces, hung inside the old barn rethinking my life, and devoured books on Abraham Lincoln to help me stave off my loneliness. Yeah, we all know

Abe was our Republican 16th president with a great sense of humor who freed the slaves and united the divided country. But beyond those monumental achievements advancing humanity, he was a self-made man who'd lived a remarkable life during his fifty-six years. I learned a lot about Lincoln and about myself. Rudderless, I dreamed of escaping to a new life and knew I needed another change of scenery.

Though temporarily ensconced in my oldest brother's barn, I knew I wouldn't live there forever. It seemed like a sauna on summer nights, and I wasn't sure if I was sleeping in a barn or an Easy-Bake oven. I'd lose a couple of pounds each night in accumulated sweat. Seth beckoned me to live with him in California again. He offered to get an apartment we could share and also guaranteed me a job at the Otto Cap factory, where he worked manufacturing hats. But I'd just returned from California. And I knew I didn't want to work in a factory making anything. For any amount of money. It just wasn't for me. I wanted to do something with my life. Find purpose. Harness my creative energy to enter into a career. Impact the world in some small way. Seth mostly just wanted to smoke pot, drink beer, and hang out at home. I didn't want to go where I believed he was headed, and he didn't want to go where he thought I was headed. We had our differences.

I pondered long and hard about where to move next, teetering on a few possible locations. I realized my decision was based on how much it would cost me to get there. I looked in my wallet. Inside was $37—the only money I had to my name. It was not a lot, but enough for gas and tolls to put me at my next destination. Suddenly, where I would go became abundantly clear, as I had just enough money to get there.

With hope for a better life, I took a leap of faith and drove south on the New Jersey Turnpike.

CHAPTER 11

Repaired Broken Men

When I arrived unannounced at my parents' apartment in Falls Church, Virginia—SURPRISE!—carrying the same duffel bag and acoustic guitar I transported from California a few months before, my mother happily greeted me. My unexpected presence seemed to make her day, which was terrific. For the first time in my life, I hadn't seen my mother in months. On the other hand, my dad made eye contact with me for a nanosecond before his eyes zoomed in on my duffel bag. He knew I was not just stopping by for a lunch visit.

My mom had an aside meeting with my father while I stood outside their apartment door in the long hallway. After a few minutes, he granted me entrance. I was relieved; I had nowhere else to go and no money to get there even if I did.

After stepping into their new abode and taking everything in, I was overcome with sadness. For nineteen years, my parents used to own a 4-bedroom, 2-bath, 1,400-square-foot Cape Cod on a tree-filled half-acre corner lot in a beautiful, suburban development in New Jersey. My mother often said that was her favorite home out of all the sixteen homes she lived in. In Virginia, she was now living in a two-bedroom rented apartment in a gritty building in a congested city outside densely populated Washington DC. No half-acre private property. No trees in the yard. People were on top of one another. Despite being an uncomfortable arrangement for my folks and me, I lived with them for about six months, sleeping on the pull-out couch in the TV room each night and folding it up every morning. That was the routine.

Soon after emptying my duffel bag, I sought employment. I decided to try something different from my previous blue-collar jobs of pumping gas, cutting lawns, painting homes, and sanding and prepping cars in an auto body shop. I scoured the local classifieds and circled ads from a few newspapers. I responded to one listing that caught my eye: a marketing company looking for someone to train. I spoke with a peppy-sounding lady named Julie. Though I tried to extract specific information about the marketing job, Julie relinquished nothing. She only wanted my information, deflecting every question I asked about the nature of the work. After getting nowhere with her but desperately needing employment, I agreed to schedule an interview with the Blaketon Marketing company the following morning. I knew I was trainable and was confident I could succeed in marketing, whatever that was.

When I entered the hotel in the Crystal City neighborhood of Arlington at the appointed time, I proceeded to the lobby area as instructed. It was packed with about forty people from all ages and walks of life milling about. Applicants' attire ranged from business suits and ties to raggedy T-shirts and jeans. The candidates seemed about as enthused as if they were there to receive a colorectal exam. I brushed off what I observed and sat beside the other workplace rejects who, like me, were lost souls struggling to find a suitable career. I sat rehearsing answers to possible interview questions, muttering to myself. Out of nowhere, a sharp-dressed, twenty-something, petite, and perky blonde named Cindy appeared and herded us into a conference room. The group quietly filed in like obedient sheep and took our seats. Cindy provided a scripted speech about how the company was Fortune 500; the top marketing reps earned a half-million dollars a year, you could retire by age forty, and everything else we wanted to hear. Who *wouldn't* want this job? Most applicants sat with glazed faces, stifling yawns and nodding along, while I and a few others enthusiastically jotted down notes. After what seemed like an eternity yet was only about thirty minutes, Cindy finally revealed to us the "amazing" and "life-changing" product Blaketon Marketing wanted us to "market."

A vacuum cleaner. [SOUND OF NEEDLE SCRATCHING A VINYL RECORD.]

Talk about a buzzkill. But according to Cindy, they weren't just any vacuum cleaners; they were Dirby's!

I was furious, as were most of the others in the room. After Cindy pulled the vacuum cleaner—which she referred to as an air purification system—from underneath the table and unveiled it to the audience, three-quarters of the people stood up. They filed out of the room in one mass exodus, grumbling as they left. Undeterred after losing most of her prospects, Cindy continued to describe the Dirby and its reported state-of-the-art features. A few more folks stood and trickled out the door as she spoke.

I would have hung up if I had been informed on the phone that Blaketon Marketing was looking for salespeople to sell vacuum cleaners door-to-door. This is precisely why the first girl I spoke with was so evasive about the nature of the work—well played on her end.

Marketing, my ass. It's cold-calling. Door-to-door sales. Trespassing on private property and then disturbing people at their homes to try and sell them an overpriced vacuum.

I wanted to get back at Cindy since she made my morning a colossal waste of time. After Cindy fielded questions from the half-dozen people in the room, I threw her a curveball. Cindy asked if there were any more questions before preparing for the next step in her sales process—the close. My hand flew up. "I have a question," I began. She pointed to me and smiled. "Why is it that John Jacob Jingleheimer Schmidt's name is my name too?" The handful of stragglers remaining in the conference room chuckled. Unable to recite a memorized answer from her recruitment training manual, Cindy stood frozen. I gathered my belongings and walked out of the conference room, shaking my head and flashing the Blaketon sales rep a departing scowl.

Vacuum cleaners. Please.

The next job ad I answered was for Encyclopedia Britannica. A longtime and reputable company, but, once again, I'd be a door-to-door salesman, cold-calling—a.k.a. disturbing people at their homes. Been there, done that as a nine-year-old selling stolen candy bars. I didn't want to knock on people's doors as an adult. So after a whopping one day of training—where I was paired with a savvy saleswoman and knocked on doors of wealthy Washingtonians—I let my supervisor know that was not the right job for me. He understood. Zero for two in my job search. I wondered if any jobs in the greater DC area did not require door-to-door sales.

Recognizing my frustration, my mother offered helpful advice by suggesting I try a different approach. She urged me to visit the F.W. Woolworth five and dime store inside the Tysons Corner Mall in McLean, Virginia, and apply for a job. Hmm. It sounded like a good idea; I liked Woolworth's. They'd been around forever, were well known, had stores across America, and sold everything. Plus, most had an old-fashioned lunch counter with red stools upon which one could perch and, in my case, order a grilled cheese sandwich, tomato soup, and a vanilla milkshake. The Woolworth lunch counters reminded me of the old Chock Full O' Nuts ones I used to frequent with my mom in Manhattan as a little boy when we'd visit her parents. Plus, Woolworth's was only a ten-minute ride from my parents' apartment where I was staying. I heeded my mom's advice, drove to Woolworth's, and filled out an application in the human resources department. After submitting my application, I was interviewed on the spot by the elderly HR director named Patricia. She was from Southern Virginia, had a strong drawl, wore glasses, and a butterfly clip tamed her hair. After a fifteen-minute back-and-forth question-and-answer session, I was hired on the spot. I was scheduled to start work the next day in the camera department. I was proud, and my mom was delighted. According to her, I secured a *real* job—where I'd get paid at the end of each week, regardless of the weather conditions or if business was slow. Though I knew almost nothing about cameras, I was paired with Rosa, who would teach me.

Rosa Velasquez was a barrel-chested, quick-witted lady from Mexico City who was about forty. She was a sweetheart who took me under her wing and taught me all I could ever want to know about cameras and film. Fun fact: Rosa taught me more Spanish than my father, who spoke the language fluently. The only thing I didn't like about my job was that I had to wear a goofy red vest with a name tag and button pinned to it, which read *The Customer Is Always Right*. I made $4.50 an hour—about a dollar more than minimum wage at the time—and was surprisingly paid in cash, handed to me in a small brown envelope each Friday afternoon. No checks to deposit, and no having to wait three business days for them to clear. There were other job perks, such as employee discounts and a climate-controlled environment in which to work. Plus, I met quality people, two of whom I keep in contact with today, some thirty-five years later. And with all the colleges nearby—George Mason University, Marymount College, Georgetown University, American University, George Washington University, NOVA, and more—there were lots of girls my age walking about the upscale two-story mall. In the eighties, malls were the places to hang out, be seen, and meet people. They were the 1980s version of social media. While most patrons who shopped at Woolworth's seemed to be septuagenarians buying doilies, Polident, canes, adult diapers, Metamucil, Chia pets, or prune juice, every once in a while, I'd see a girl my age strolling about the aisles, which was always a treat. However, it was not easy trying to gain favorable attention from such a young lady when wearing a bright red vest when your store manager stops by and orders you to dump the trash, sweep the floor, and straighten your name tag as you're in mid-conversation trying to impress the girl. Whatever cool you try to exude disappears instantly.

Working at Tysons Corner, I learned that some girls had placed a hierarchy among the stores in the mall. They seemed to like boys who worked in the more distinguished stores such as Nordstrom's, Herman's Sporting Goods, Hecht's, and Bloomingdale's—although every guy I knew who worked at "Bloomies" was gay. I learned that Woolworth's ranked near the bottom of their pecking order list, just above working in bail bonds offices, pawn shops, mini marts, cigarette outlets, adult book stores, roadside fireworks stands, check cashing places, and K-Marts and Walmarts. Oh, well. At least *I* thought it was cool. And speaking of cool . . .

There was one cute girl my age who worked in the Woolworth's restaurant called Harvest House who caught my eye. Her name was Maureen Zokolowski, and she was a waitress. Every work day during the summer of 1984, I sat at the same padded red stool at the end of the counter and ordered from her a grilled cheese sandwich, tomato soup, and a vanilla shake for lunch. Maureen got a kick out of my order, and I enjoyed her company and smile. I found her to be interesting and fun.

Maureen attended MIT in Cambridge, Massachusetts, studying astrophysics and was home for the summer. (She was one of the "intelligent girls" I "always seem to date," according to my mother, mentioned in this book's Prologue.) Maureen lived in upscale Langley and came from a wealthy, supportive family who adored her. Her dad was an FBI agent, and her mother was a diplomat to either Lichtenstein or Luxembourg. I'm not sure which one. I always get them confused with each other.

Maureen's family operated as a functional, happy, and cohesive unit. They were normal. This was contrary to my dysfunctional, fragmented, unhappy, and abnormal family. After experiencing my dysfunctional family and my ex-girlfriend Diane's dysfunctional family, it was like being handed an oxygen mask after inhaling nothing but toxic fumes for years. Upon first developing a friendship with Maureen, we began seeing each other as boyfriend and girlfriend. Evidently, the girl was OK dating a moron. My mother liked Maureen and wondered why she chose to date me. So, I did my best to keep the two apart. That way, my mother could not embarrass me by asking Maureen why she was dating her son rather than one of those intelligent boys up at MIT.

Maureen was a cool, intelligent, and sweet girl who taught me it was possible to trust again. After a tumultuous two-year relationship dating a strumpet, I used to wonder if all girls were cheats like Diane. But Maureen proved it was not the case. I found myself a good girl again. It was like experiencing a warm sunbeam on my body after two years of enduring continuous gray skies, cold rain, and pounding hail.

Maureen and I spent our free time together riding my new Suzuki GS 550L motorcycle around Northern Virginia, the scenic Shenandoah Valley, and the Blue Ridge Mountains. The bike was made possible by steady pay from my 'real' job at Woolworth's. Aside from motorcycle riding, Maureen and I drove around the greater DC area in my recently purchased red 1971 Karmann Ghia convertible, also courtesy of my steady job. We visited DC museums and historical monuments and played on the Woolworth's softball team I organized, challenging other stores' teams from the Tysons Corner Mall. We were young, enthusiastic, full of energy and curiosity. We had a blast living during the mid-1980s, a highly prosperous and much less divisive time in America where everyone seemed to get along. Aside from my budding relationship with Maureen, I also made friends with those who worked at Woolworth's.

John Sherman was a cerebral guy and talented athlete who was an engineering student at Michigan State. Like Maureen, John worked at Woolworth's on school breaks throughout the year and in the summer. He reminded me of my high school Honor Roll friend, Patrick Walsh. They were both bright and athletic and on track to become highly successful in whatever career they chose.

Pete Herndon was my age, a gifted artist with a great sense of humor and, like me, a fellow Beatlemaniac. Plus, like me, Pete was a lost soul. Both friends liked my new girlfriend, Maureen, and Maureen liked my new friends. We'd all hang out on weekends in Georgetown or George Mason University bars. On weeknights when we weren't working, my guy friends and I would play pick-up basketball games at Northern Virginia school gyms. That was a time when people could do such a thing at their local elementary schools or high schools. Good luck finding that today. You'd be met with padlocks, chains, and ominous notices posted to every door warning you to keep out.

After a few months of assisting in the small camera department at Woolworth's, I was promoted to the much larger sporting goods department. Sporting goods comprised about one-sixth of the massive store's square footage, and the aisles were often teeming with eager shoppers bustling about. It was a coveted position within the retail giant. For a Jersey boy who had never held a rifle, shotgun, or crossbow in his hands, I was now tasked to sell them. While the sporting goods department sold traditional items such as various balls, bats, gloves, camping, hunting, fishing, and hiking equipment, most of my customers shopped for firearms and other weapons. It was an enjoyable new experience, and in no time, I became knowledgeable about the products I was enthusiastically selling.

After three months and a proliferation in sales, the store manager approached me again and promoted me to sporting goods manager. That act made me beam with pride. People recognized my efforts and appreciated my achievements. I was unused to such recognition. The promotion came with a pay raise to $5.50 an hour to compensate me for my increased responsibilities of ordering merchandise, supervising part-time workers, coordinating schedules, training new hires, and more. Everything was going along so well at Woolworth's. I could not believe all of my good fortunes. I felt my life had a purpose for the first time in years. I fit in and felt a sense of belonging, which was the first time I felt that. It was overwhelming. My coworkers and customers looked forward to seeing me; and me them. I was not only visible at Woolworth's; I was highly visible. While I missed my hometown friends up in New Jersey, I made good friends down in Virginia. Life was enjoyable again. What a welcomed relief.

During the fifteen months I lived in Virginia between ages twenty and twenty-one, for nine weeks, I had a friend live with me, err . . . my *parents* and me, in their small apartment in Falls Church.

Danny Weber was a nationally-ranked runner on my former high school track team. He was a New Jersey state champion in the mile run yet had recently fallen upon hard times after getting involved with cocaine in college. Danny was booted from Division 1 powerhouse Auburn University in Alabama, blowing his full track scholarship. Future professional multi-sport phenom Bo Jackson was attending Auburn at the same time. Danny and Bo knew each other, having been highly acclaimed recruits for the university's track program. While Danny competed in the one-mile race, Bo competed as a sprinter, hurdler, jumper (long jump & high jump), thrower (discus, shot put), and decathlon. An athletic anomaly, Bo also played college baseball and football at Auburn, two sports where he would eventually gain fame.

On a visit to Geneva to see hometown friends one weekend, I noticed Danny drunk and high on cocaine at a party. He had white powder on his nose and was more hyped up than a squirrel on amphetamines. It was shocking to see. Danny never drank, never smoked cigarettes, and never did any drugs in high school. He shunned those vices. His high had always been running. "There's Danny running!" folks proudly said, pointing to the lean young man as he trotted by their homes. Back then, if you could ever get Danny to stop running and talk to you, he'd only do so while jogging in place. He was a superb athlete and jolly guy, and the last person in the world I thought would involve himself with drugs. But there he was at the party, coked-up, smoking cigarettes, and chugging alcohol. It was a sad sight. And I felt compelled to intervene.

I offered Danny an opportunity to escape the quicksand I knew our hometown could easily swallow him up in and move down to Virginia to live with me and my parents.

I didn't do drugs, I told him, so there would be no temptation for him. It would be a safe environment, especially since I'd grown out of my mischief stage. I knew he'd have fun, as we always got along well.

After mulling over the offer for a day, Danny gladly accepted my invitation. I called my mother and asked for her blessing to help a friend in need. She opened up her heart and her apartment home to Danny. She also got my father on board with the idea. What I'm sure helped is everybody in our hometown knew and liked Danny. He was a local sports prodigy. The kid was second only to my best friend Anthony as the most likable person in my age group from my hometown.

I shared the small second bedroom with Danny—he was on the cot, and I was on the couch. With Danny's well-documented athletic credentials, he was instantly hired to sell running shoes at Herman's Sporting Goods behind the Tysons Corner Mall. It was a perfect match. Danny drove a yellow VW Bug and I drove my red VW Karmann Ghia convertible to work and around town. During those nine weeks, the former New Jersey State Champion ran every morning and night and, most importantly, became drug-free. No 12-step program, just Cold Turkey.

We enjoyed our time together while we had it: sightseeing, meeting new people, and visiting new places in and around the greater DC region. I was glad to help my fellow lost soul get back on track—no pun intended. His decision to join me in Virginia was a wise one. I was incredibly proud of my mother for allowing Danny to reclaim his once-excellent life. I was also proud of my father for agreeing to the arrangement. A few months before, my dad and I came to blows in our former New Jersey home. Though we barely spoke to each other, I could see the move down to Virginia did him well. He found full-time work in computer programming and cleaned up his act with his drinking. He'd still have a few beers now and then after work at home sitting in front of the TV, and then on Saturday nights when he and my mother visited Squire Rockwell's in Annandale to watch their favorite cover band perform. But that was it. Although there were a handful of chapters of the American Legion in the greater DC area, my father never set foot in any of them. He prospered with work and appeared he'd finally found peace in his life.

After one year, my parents' apartment lease was up, and they decided to buy a condo in Burke, about twenty minutes south of where they were living in Falls Church. When they moved, Danny returned to New Jersey to hit the reset button on his life. Like many drug addicts and alcoholics struggling to regain control of their existence, Danny became a born-again Christian. I guess he needed to do that to stay clean. Thankfully, thirty-plus years later, he's still clean. Without a doubt, that is his life's greatest accomplishment.

Although it was a longer commute, I enjoyed the Burke condo, having my own bedroom, and Burke itself much more than the crowded Falls Church. My parents' condo was much larger than their former apartment and was new, updated, and *theirs*. They owned it. The residents of their new condo community treated the grounds and property with respect. They took pride in home ownership, unlike the many renting slobs in their former apartment complex who tossed trash on the lobby floor, littered in the parking lot, didn't replace burned-out light bulbs, kept junk on their patios or decks, and left children's toys strewn about the grounds. Burke was more upscale. It had a lake, and I enjoyed fishing and driving a motorboat around in it. And Burke had plenty of winding roads ideally suited to riding my motorcycle. Plus, it was less congested than Falls Church, where sprawling blocks of hi-rise apartments, worn-out strip malls, gas stations, and minimarts dotted the landscape.

GRAY SKIES: A (Moron's) Memoir

At the end of 1985, I received interesting news from Woolworth's corporate office in Manhattan. The company brass wanted to promote me to the management training program. It was an intensive, four-month apprentice operation upon which completing I would run my own store. They suggested Maryland, Ohio, or West Virginia as possible locations to transfer to. I was honored that they thought of me in such a good light. I was only twenty-one. A little over a year before, I was a confused kid sitting in the Tysons Corner Mall Woolworth's, nervously filling out an application to work an entry-level job, clueless about what I wanted to do with my life. Now, the most successful five-and-dime operation in world history wanted me to run my own store. The offer blew my mind. I was just twenty-one. let corporate know I'd accept under one condition—they gave me a New Jersey store.

After a few days of getting down to the nitty-gritty of logistics, matters were finalized. Thankfully, the company granted my request. I was given a small store to manage in Milltown, New Jersey. I called my buddy Anthony, a junior at Trenton State College at the time, and told him the good news. He congratulated me and, without hesitation, offered me half the space in his bedroom within the small rowhome he was renting off-campus with another TSC student. It was an incredibly generous offer, and I gladly accepted it. Two childhood friends from the old neighborhood reconnecting was a great thing. When I eventually visited the home, I discovered Anthony was already sharing his tiny bedroom with his gorgeous new TSC girlfriend, Isabella. Anthony never said a word about the arrangement. I felt awful for him and his new girlfriend because I would be the third body crammed into their tight space. A dresser shoe-horned in the middle of the room, acting as the room divider between us, made matters even more challenging. I didn't know if a twin mattress would fit on the floor. Since my sleeping area would be the size of a coffin, I considered sleeping standing up for the first time. Horses, zebras, and elephants did it; why couldn't humans?

My place of residence-to-be was a scruffy, urban rowhome in a neighborhood teeming with poverty and crime, but it was affordable at $117 a month for my share. In addition, it was only a thirty-five-minute drive straight up Route One north to my new store.

I shared my promotion, transfer, and move to New Jersey news with my girlfriend, Maureen. She was supportive and happy. I'd be closer to her in Cambridge, where she was a junior at M.I.T.—an easy five-hour train ride from Trenton.

I bought a new, red 1986 Ford Escort for $7,400, packed my belongings, drove 4 hours to Trenton, and instantly settled into my new home and job. Two weeks later, on my first day off from Woolworth's, I trained down to Virginia to retrieve my motorcycle.

I just turned twenty-two and was a manager-in-training at Woolworth's, working under the direction of Mr. Bob Orson, the longtime manager of the Milltown location. Mr. Orson was tall and wiry with a body incapable of keeping still. When he spoke, his ridiculously long arms constantly flailed about like those tall promotional inflatable puppets you see on car dealership lots. He was a standup guy soon to retire, so my arrival at that store came as a relief to him, a forty-year employee of the F. W. Woolworth Company.

Happy ending here, right? I ride off into the sunset in my new Ford Escort and enjoy a successful forty-year career working as a retail variety store manager for Woolworth's. Not so fast.

After four months, it became clear that I did not want to be a Woolworth's store manager. I wanted out. A confluence of factors contributed to my decision to leave the company.

First, I enjoyed interacting with customers. It was what I loved most about my job and partly earned me recognition in the company. It helped me quickly rise through the ranks—from camera department clerk to sporting goods worker to sporting goods manager to store manager, all within fifteen months. In Virginia, customers often made it a point to seek out the store manager to praise my helpful and friendly ways. One satisfied customer even wrote a letter commending my work and mailed it to one of the corporate bigwigs who worked in the famous Woolworth Building in Manhattan. (I still have a copy of that letter!) The challenge I faced as a store manager was I had almost no time to interact with customers on the sales floor. Though I was regularly peppered with questions from our loyal shoppers, upper management discouraged me from mingling with them. The corporate muckety-mucks wanted me to focus more on product inventory management, employee scheduling, advertising, banking, human resources, and more. More time in the back office crunching numbers and speaking with district and regional managers on the phone and less time walking around the sales floor interacting with customers. That was contradictory to who I was. I *needed* human interaction and thrived on it.

Second, I was pulled in a dozen directions every moment of the day, fielding never-ending questions while maintaining a modicum of order amidst the chaos.

- "Mr. K? I need register tape up at register one. . ."
- "A delivery truck is here, Mr. K. Do you want me to help you unload it?"

- "Mr. K? The malted milk mixer at the lunch counter broke. Gladys doesn't know how to fix it. Can you help her?"
- "Mr. K, an angry customer is on the phone, saying the toilet seat she bought here broke. She wants her money back. Can you speak with her?"
- "I need more nickels and dimes in register three up front, Mr. K! I'm out."
- "Attention: clean up in aisle six. Mop and cone needed in aisle six."
- "Mr. K, that mentally disturbed homeless guy is the one we caught shoplifting here a few times. Can you get him to leave again? He's also the one who craps all over the bathroom floor and doesn't clean up his mess."
- "Mr. K! The bathroom toilet is clogged and won't flush. The plunger's not working. It's disgusting in there. Can you please help?"
- "Mr. K? A customer broke a light bulb in aisle seven. She offered to pay for it. What should I do?"
- "Mr. K? I need singles and fives up front at register two."
- "The freight bell is ringing in the stockroom, Mr. K. Another delivery truck is here."
- "Mr. K? I can't work tomorrow. My friend's cousin got tickets to see Twisted Sister in New York, and we're heading to the city all day."
- "Mr. K? Jimmy hasn't shown up for his shift to relieve me. Can you call him to find out where he is? He should've been here fifteen minutes ago. This is his third tardy this week . . ."
- "Mr. K? Can I switch my hours with Megan on Mondays and Wednesdays for the next few weeks? Megan said if she can get Valerie or Harris to cover for

her and you're OK with it, I'd prefer those days. It's kind of an emergency."
- "Mr. K? You have a call from corporate about last month's numbers. Can you take it?"
- "Mr. K? A woman named Harriet would like to exchange her pink doilies for the white ones, but we don't have white ones in stock. What should she do?"
- "Mr. K? Someone wants to see the manager about job openings. Are you available to meet with her?"
- "One of the parakeets died, Mr. K. What do I do with it?" [NOTE: I could not fathom why Woolworth's sold live exotic birds in that little store, but we did.]

. . . And countless other things.

It was sensory overload. Insanity. And responsibility, stress, and aggravation way beyond my pay grade.

Third, despite my promotion, I was actually earning *less money* than I previously did as the sporting goods department manager in the Tysons Corner store. How is that possible? I'll tell you.

As the sporting goods manager in Virginia, I worked forty hours a week and was paid $5.50 an hour. That's $220 a week, $11,400 a year for a much more fun and much less stressful job. In my "promotion" to store manager in New Jersey, I was paid $14,000 a year, yet I was required to work at least *sixty* hours a week. Some weeks, I worked seventy hours or more. So I was earning about $4.50 an hour—a dollar LESS per hour than I was making as sporting goods department manager. Plus, I was driving farther and using more gas commuting. That all factored in.

Fourth, I had no interest in becoming one of those guys who worked seventy-hour weeks over forty years to wake up one day pushing sixty-five—yet look eighty—and wonder where my life had gone. Being a hamster on a wheel never interested me. No disrespect to hamsters or retail variety store managers, of course. It just wasn't in my DNA.

Lastly, I didn't want other people in control of my life; I wanted to be the one holding the reins. I didn't want to settle in at the Woolworth store in New Jersey and be told eight months later that corporate wants me to run a Woolworth's in Minnesota, Illinois, Oregon, or Florida. And then two years later be transferred to a Woolworth's in Maine. And then once I got acclimated to that New England store, be assigned to a Woolworth's in California. Don't get me wrong; I liked to travel and experience new places and meet new people. But only on my terms—not when someone else dictates where and when to go. But that is the way of the retail world. You could eventually make a six-figure annual salary in that career if you were willing to work tirelessly and be transferred anywhere at any time. I wasn't interested in being a pinball, bounced around by forces beyond my control. I just turned twenty-two. I was a free spirit. Like most guys that age, I wanted to hang with my friends, take a weekend off to enjoy mindless fun, meet girls, and get laid. And have less responsibility. Shocking, I know.

So after working six months for the small Woolworth's in Milltown, New Jersey—the last two months running the store entirely alone—I put in for my two-week paid vacation. It was granted. I headed to California—on my terms—to see my odd friend Seth, who had been bugging me to visit.

I enjoyed two fantastic weeks out in California, and I returned to Jersey decompressed and with a clear mind. Once back at work, I called the corporate office and spoke to my district manager to verbally give him my official one-month notice, backing up that verbal announcement with an official resignation letter I typed and faxed to him. I thanked Woolworth's for the great memories and the opportunity they provided me over the last two years, and most of all, for believing in a directionless young man who often didn't believe in himself. My resignation was accepted, but only after the corporate office asked me to reconsider.

I figured out what I *didn't* want to do for a living—be a retail variety store manager. Yet, I had no idea what I wanted to do. I had time to figure that out. My time at Woolworth's taught me I could be a success at anything I put my mind to. It was as if a switch had been turned on inside my head, lighting up a new world of possibilities.

As I pondered my future, I thought of painting homes again as a business owner instead of working for someone else. I knew there was good money to be made as the owner, and the work was uncomplicated. And it provided freedom.

I also considered getting into the developing and financially lucrative pharmaceutical sales industry. People at Woolworth's often told me I was a great communicator, which has long been the bedrock of sales success.

Maybe I'd attend school to become an audio engineer and help musicians record their albums.

Perhaps I'd see if my oldest brother wanted to expand his auto body business to include me. We could open several shops throughout New Jersey, and I could run a location.

Then again, I thought about working with children. Maybe I'd serve youth who needed to be uplifted. I could be a positive male role model to kids without fathers or underdogs with disengaged dads.

Perhaps I'd provide guitar lessons for a living or reunite The Boys to play some gigs. Who knew? I was so young then. There were endless possibilities. Unlike just a few years before—when I had a dim idea of my future—I looked forward to traveling the roads to discover my life. I was empowered to move forward with a new sense of confidence and determination to make something of myself. I believed there were blue and sunny skies ahead. No more gray skies.

CHAPTER 12

Farewell

ABOUT MY FRIENDS ...

Not many people can say they've maintained the same friends for forty or fifty years. Well, I can. Though I've made several close friends over the last few decades, I still count Mehmet, Anthony, Michael, Joel, Dave, Patrick, and others as my brothers. They're longer in the tooth, fuller in the waistline, have less hair on their heads, and most have children and even grandchildren. I hope to continue my friendship/brotherhood with these Jersey boys for the next fifty years.

Sadly, I lost my oldest friend, Michael Michaels, who had been struggling with drug addiction for decades. When I heard the news, I was crushed. It was like a part of my heart had been ripped out. Our many childhood memories made together can never again be shared with one another. He's gone. I often think about him. I miss him.

A childhood friend recently told me he "loved me like a brother." I raised my hands as if to stop traffic and told him not to say that; instead, tell me he loves me like a *friend*. That way, I'd know our relationship would continue.

ABOUT MY SIBLINGS...

My sister—thirteen years my senior—and I have the same relationship now that we did fifty years ago, forty years ago, ten years ago, five years ago, and last year. We don't speak.

Due to several events that occurred years ago, Brother 1 and I rarely see and speak to each other.

Brother 2 and I do speak and see each other, but rarely. Not due to any falling out but because it's always been that way. He's a man of few words and not a good communicator. He never was. If I call Brother 2, he'll talk for a minute, then hand the phone to his wife or say he's got to go. Communication is painful to him. In that regard, he is my father. He's never initiated a call to me. Ever. Sad, but true.

Years ago, my wife and I drove through a small town in America's Great Plains. It was a place with limited restaurant options, so our best choice was the Olive Garden. After being seated at our booth by the hostess, our server cheerily greeted us. Before he could fire off his corporate-mandated script, I asked him if he could summon the manager. The server tilted his head and asked if there was a problem. I said no, I just wanted to ask the manager a question. A minute later, the bewildered manager appeared. I said hello and asked her if the Olive Garden's motto was still *'When you're here, you're family.'* Even more confused now, she confirmed that it was. I smiled and asked her when I should start arguing with the workers— before or after the meal?

ABOUT MY MOTHER . . .

The week before my 41st birthday, my otherwise healthy and spunky mother was admitted to her local hospital for a routine procedure to replace the battery in her pacemaker. Her cardiologist said it would be "a twenty-minute, simple outpatient procedure."

It wasn't.

Over six grueling days, my mother died a slow and agonizing death in that same hospital due to her cardiologist's later admitted mistakes during that supposed "simple procedure."

My mother was my lone protector growing up, my guardian, and the only one in my family who seemed to give a shit about me, so I cannot fully describe how devastated I was upon her passing. Those who've lost a loving parent know. As the sole caretaker for my father—who at the time had slipped into the clutches of Alzheimer's disease—my mother still had a lot of life left in her when her cardiologist cut her life short. I think about her every day, and I miss her. I'd give just about anything to spend one more day with her. I'd even take her questioning my intelligence or why it took me so long to get my college degrees. While my mother got to know the kooky kid with the finicky appetite she raised, I wish she could have gotten to know the good man he eventually became. She missed so much that I think she would have been proud of. I often see little old ladies in their eighties or nineties shuffling about, assisted by their rollator walkers. I stare at them, envious of their ages and wishing my mother had reached that length of life so I could have spent more time with her.

ABOUT MY FATHER . . .

The last time I saw my father, he was lying in a New Jersey hospital bed during the final days of his life, three years after my mother's death. He was frail, weak, and vulnerable—three things he never was during my childhood. He appeared hollowed out, perhaps by illness or just from life itself. But he was awake and had his dark brown eyes fixed on me as I stood at the foot of his gurney. Not once did my father glance at my beautiful wife standing beside me. He did not take his eyes off me despite not a spoken word between us. I found that ironic. In my life, my father rarely put his eyes on me; on his deathbed, he couldn't take them off me. I glanced at my wife to see if she noticed what was happening.

She had.

When I moved slightly to the left, my father's eyes followed. When I took a few steps to the right, his eyes stayed on me. They were the same dark brown eyes that used to look at me menacingly and instilled great fear in me as a child. My wife suggested it may have been his way of taking me in for a final time before he passed or his way of apologizing for not being a great father during years gone by. I had no response to either thought. I tried to process the magnitude of the moment. It was overwhelming. Even in his diminished state, I hoped he would mouth the words *I'm sorry* or *I'm proud of you* or *I love you* so that I could experience it just once in my life. As the eternal optimist, I always believed that one day he would. But my father said nothing.

Though I was still angry and wounded from a lifetime of hurt, I pulled up a chair beside his bed and sidled up close to my father. I grabbed his hand and held it in mine as we locked eyes. His long fingers were like twigs. I felt like if I had squeezed his hand with even minimal force, I could have shattered his long fingers to pieces. Staring at him with my mother's baby blues, I told him that I loved him, forgave him, and was sorry for whatever I did that made him not love me.

His eyes still on me, my father remained silent.

I bent down and kissed him on his olive-skinned forehead. And then I left the hospital, my wife in tow.

The next afternoon, Brother 1 called me to let me know my father drew his last breath.

For decades, I had longed for my dad to say *I love you* or *I'm proud of you, Michael,* just once to me. As long as he was alive, there was always hope and the possibility that he would one day. But I'd never get to hear him say those words. He was gone for good.

It took me decades to understand the complexities of our relationship—or lack thereof—as father and son. Though he was not a good father to me, I realized he was not a bad man.

In our contemporary society, I'm struck by how many people make excuses for bad behavior committed by men who grew up poor, without fathers, and raised by single mothers. These men are given free passes to commit any crimes they wish. And if caught, they go unpunished because of the harsh circumstances under which they were raised.

Well, my father also grew up poor. Dirt poor, in fact. And he, too, was raised with no dad around. His father abandoned him before my father was born. My dad was not even lucky enough to be raised by his mother. She was not around either. Both of his parents abandoned him. He was raised by his aunt and uncle, two kind souls who stepped up to raise a lost and unwanted child. If all that wasn't enough of a challenge, my father grew up during the Great Depression—America's worst financial crisis, lasting over a decade.

While he did not become the best husband or father in the world, my father did not rob, rape, shoot, loot, car-jack, or murder anyone. He never joined a gang. Nor did he sell drugs that killed or crippled countless people with addiction. My father had no criminal record. And at no point in his life did he choose to indiscriminately impregnate multiple different women and sire scores of unwanted children he'd abandon—the majority of whom would grow up to continue the cycle, as empirical data has proven over generations.

Before my father married, he stayed out of trouble and away from drugs and alcohol. He studied, got A's in high school, graduated college with honors, briefly attended medical school, went to work, got married, and started a family—in that order. I think about this every time I hear a criminal goes unpunished and is excused after his twentieth, fiftieth, or one hundred and fifth (that's an actual number!) criminal arrest because he grew up poor and without a father. So, in that sense, my father was a life success. He overcame his harsh beginnings despite the odds stacked against him.

ABOUT MY PARENTS ...

Shortly after my father passed away, my siblings and I had a family meeting to divide up my parents' life belongings. Rather than finding items that held monetary value—like one sibling—I focused on looking for things of sentimental value.

I was rummaging through some musty old boxes when I came upon an archaic tin box containing dozens of dusty old cards and love letters. My mom and dad wrote them to each other between 1947 and 1950 while they were dating. The letters were marinated in the scent of pipe tobacco, courtesy of my maternal grandfather's passion, which he stored in that box.

Upon reading the first few letters, I was misty-eyed. They were passionately and beautifully written, and I could see and feel that, at one time, my parents deeply loved one another and enjoyed each other's company. They couldn't stand the thought of being apart—even if for only a day. It blew me away.

It turns out my angry and sullen dad was once a sweet-talking lovebird, head over heels in love with my blue-eyed, blonde-haired, bobbysoxer mother. My devoted mother thought the same of my father; he was her knight in shining armor. She said so herself in her letters to him.

I guess what made them drift apart during their fifty-five-year marriage was their four children and the various burdens we created for them. My sister was born in 1951, and their last love letter was dated 1950. You do the math.

EPILOGUE

This book offers a small sampling of embarrassing and agonizing moments from my youth, included here for your reading pleasure. Through all these harrowing times, I never would have guessed that I'd one day meet my best friend, marry her, and enjoy my incredible life with the woman.

    My wife and I have traveled extensively, lived around the country, enjoyed unique experiences, met many interesting people—both famous and unknown—and made solid friends. We've struggled with the deaths of loved ones, several health scares, and many other challenges life has thrown at us. We started strong nearly three decades ago, yet we've grown even stronger as the years have passed.

    My story affirms that no matter where you start in life is not necessarily where you have to end up. Every now and then along the journey, a ray of sunshine will peek through the clouds and show you the way.

ACKNOWLEDGEMENTS

Thanks to my beautiful wife, who has always believed in me and supported my endeavors. Without her encouragement, this book would still be an idea swirling inside my rock-free head. This wonderful life could not have been possible without her, and I would not be the man I am without her. She is an angel and my life's greatest treasure.

Thanks also to the people who helped shape my journey—from friends and family and coaches to negative influencers and nonbelievers to those who extended a helping hand to me in times of need.

A special thanks to Ernest Anthony, who was always there to lift me up when I was down.

ABOUT THE AUTHOR

Despite his mother thinking he was a moron as a teenager—due to a combination of his poor grades in high school and his buffoonery—as a working adult, Mike Kelly earned his bachelor's degree and master's degree, both with honors.

Pursuant to leaving a successful career in public relations, Mike chose to serve the nonprofit world, where he became a New Jersey State award-winning transition educator serving kids with disabilities. He has published three books: *Special Stories: Short Stories On Youth With Disabilities And My Adventures Working In The Disabilities Field*, *Technical Difficulties*, and *Gray Skies*. He's working on his next book, a novel entitled *With Hope Comes Pain*.

Mike's interests include music, travel, history, MMA, and helping underdog kids.

Other books by Mike Kelly

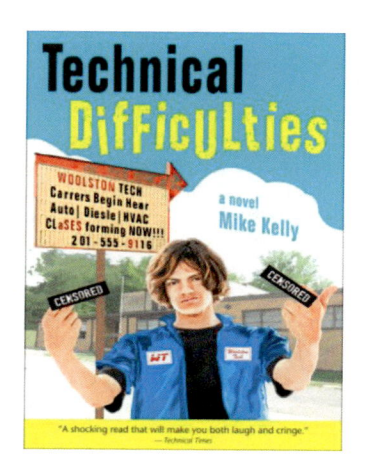

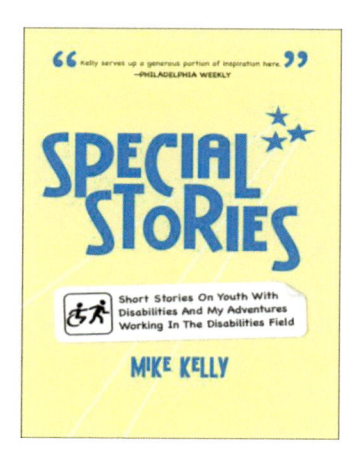

Visit **www.venduebooks.com** for more info on Mike Kelly's books.